A CHRISTIAN FAITH FOR TODAY

Most people today accept that we live in a world regulated by the laws of natural science. But how should Christian believers reconcile the divine mysteries of faith and incarnation with established empirical knowledge, whilst leaving space for a loving and intelligent creator?

A *Christian Faith for Today* provides both Christians and sceptics with a much-needed response to modernity's challenge to God. Returning to the biblical stories and sources that endure as the basis of modern faith, and to fundamental theological problems such as the divinity and humanity of Jesus, it suggests how the miraculous might be received and understood from a rational perspective, and the genuinely transcendental distinguished from narrative allegory and symbolism. From one of the world's foremost religious authorities, this is a timely and sensitive exposition of God's manifestation and intervention in the world, and of his purposes with us and for us, set out in terms sympathetic to the gospel yet acceptable to the modern mind.

W. Montgomery Watt is a world authority on religion who has held professorships at the Universities of Edinburgh, Toronto and Georgetown and the Collège de France. He is a priest of the Scottish Episcopalian Church, and has published over 30 books on Christianity and Islam.

A CHRISTIAN FAITH FOR TODAY

W. MONTGOMERY WATT

London and New York

First published 2002 by Routledge
11 New Fetter Lane, London EC4P 4EE

Simultaneously published in the USA and Canada
by Routledge
29 West 35th Street, New York, NY 10001

Routledge is an imprint of the Taylor & Francis Group

© 2002 W. Montgomery Watt

Designed and typeset in Eras and Novarese by
Keystroke, Jacaranda Lodge, Wolverhampton
Printed and bound in Great Britain
by Biddles Ltd, Guildford and King's Lynn

British Library Cataloguing in Publication Data
A catalogue record for this book is available from the British Library

Library of Congress Cataloging in Publication Data
A catalog record for this book has been requested

ISBN 0–415–27702–7 (hbk)
ISBN 0–415–27703–5 (pbk)

CONTENTS

INTRODUCTION ONE

This book is an attempt to present the truth incorporated in the Christian religion in a form which is not incompatible with the dominant intellectual outlook at the present day. This outlook is largely determined by the conception of the world achieved by the natural sciences. Most people now accept the fact that we live in a world in which things occur in accordance with fixed natural laws. This implies that there can be no such things as miracles, if these are regarded as breaches of natural law; but the Bible presents many such miracles in both Old and New Testaments. In many cases these are said to have been brought about by God interfering with natural processes. For instance it is said that God caused the sun to stand still in the sky for a whole day to enable Joshua and his men to effect a complete rout of his enemies (Joshua 10.13). The form in which this is described is based on the view that the sun moves round the earth; but, even if it is translated into terms of the earth moving round the sun, it is completely unacceptable to the modern mind that the rotation of the earth should be slowed down or stopped. Since modern Christians cannot accept any such assertion, it is necessary for them to reconsider all the alleged miracles.

In this world of fixed natural laws it is also difficult to see how there can be a place for a loving and intelligent being able to have some influence over events, and even over events in human lives. Some people would think that at most it would be possible for such a being to give human beings an experience of some spiritual presence with them, but little more. Yet Christianity asserts that underlying this universe in which we live, and in some respects operative in it, is something like a human mind, will and purpose. This is God whose existence is asserted in the Christian creeds. The following pages are an attempt to formulate the main assertions of the creeds in terms acceptable to the modern mind.

THE NATURE OF TRUTH   TWO

In order to deal with the problems raised by the contemporary intellectual outlook it is necessary for religious believers to spend some time first of all considering the nature of truth. This means looking at the different ways in which truth may be expressed, and how religious and scientific truth are related to one another. At the present time many people seem to think that the only form of truth is literal or factual truth, but this is far from the case. It is not literally true that 'the Lord is my shepherd', but it is nevertheless true in a profound sense. Truth in general is a quality of verbal statements. A statement is true when what it presents to our minds is something real, that is, something which really exists or is an aspect of reality. The presentation, however, can be made in different ways, as will now be shown.

It is also important to realize that the human mind has serious limitations. There are many matters, even in the natural world, of which we can form only an imperfect idea. We know a lot about electricity, but we can form no clear image of what electricity is in itself. Similarly we know a lot about gas and gases but can form no clear image. The idea of life, again, is in much the same position; it is something with which we are very familiar in its many forms, but we have no clear image to represent it, only a word. Likewise in the religious sphere we can form no clear image of God, but this in itself does not make God unreal, as is shown by these other examples.

We should likewise be aware how the words in our languages have different meanings. When our early forefathers with simple forms of life developed a language, the words in it referred to what they were familiar with – material objects and their qualities, actions and movements, relationships and the like. We now describe these words as nouns, adjectives, verbs, adverbs, prepositions, conjunctions. These are the basic words in a language. When people wanted to speak about something for which there was no basic word, they might sometimes invent a new word, but mostly they used an existing word in a secondary sense. Thus they came to speak of a river running, because it was doing something like what a man or an animal does. A great many words are now used in this secondary way. Because English has incorporated many words from Latin and Greek we do not always recognize secondary usages as such. When we speak of the 'current' of a river, however, we are simply using a word for 'running' derived from the Latin *currere*. This applies even to high-sounding theological terms like 'transcendent' and 'immanent', for these are only saying that God is 'above' or 'beyond' other things or 'dwelling' in them.

When words are used in a secondary sense this is sometimes spoken of as 'metaphorical' or 'analogical'; and 'analogical' is a term used in much Christian theology. In general no objection can be taken to these words, but for less theologically minded Christians they are perhaps best avoided, since they might suggest that what is spoken of in this way is unreal, although there is no genuine basis for such a suggestion; there is nothing unreal about the running or current of a river. It is often helpful to speak of what is being referred to by words in a secondary sense as 'something like' what is referred to in the primary sense. Thus the Christian believer in God can say that he is 'something like' a human father.

It is appropriate here to note that when words are being used in a secondary sense, the contradictions between the primary senses of these words do not necessarily apply. God's being 'something like' a father does not prevent him being also 'something like' a mother. His being transcendent does not prevent him from also being immanent. This point is especially relevant when religions are being compared, for here words are being used not merely in a secondary sense, but also in different intellectual frameworks. When the outstanding Christian theologian Thomas Merton met Buddhist monks and discussed spiritual matters with them, he and they found they had much in common despite the neglect or denial of the existence of God in the Buddhist religion.

Let us now look at the different ways in which truth may be presented.

First there is *literal truth*, which might also be called factual truth. Statements are literally true when they present matters of general knowledge in a straightforward way. This is the case even when a statement includes words in a secondary sense, as when we say that 'rivers run into the sea'. People are said to be literal-minded when they assume that all verbal statements are to be taken in this way. On the whole our contemporaries tend to be more literal-minded than previous generations. This is probably due to the vast amount of knowledge derived from the natural sciences.

From literal truth we may distinguish *symbolic truth*. This seems to have been more appreciated in New Testament times than it is at the present day. One of the chief examples is John, the writer of the fourth gospel. He selects seven events in the life of Jesus as 'signs' (*semeia*) of his achievements, and in the forefront of these, as the first of the signs, he places the changing of water into wine at Cana (John 2). Jesus was at a wedding feast with some of his disciples, and his mother was there too. When his mother said to him that the wine was running out, he told the servants to fill six large vessels with water, and then to take some and offer it to the master of the feast. When the latter tasted it, he pronounced it excellent wine, and asked the bridegroom why he had kept the best wine until this point. If the story is taken literally, it has nothing to do with the gospel. The Authorized Version's use of the word 'firkin' as a measure of the water/wine conceals the amount. The vessels together contained about 150 gallons or 900 of our standard wine bottles. Producing a vast quantity of wine is clearly not a 'sign' of the achievement of Jesus. John clearly thought of it symbolically as a sign of the ability of Jesus to transform something ordinary and humdrum into something rich and precious, namely, to bring to individuals and to the Jewish people as a whole a more profound form of religion. The words 'you have kept the best wine until now' also have a deep symbolic sense in relation to the mission of Jesus.

Many other matters in the gospels may also have been understood symbolically, and Jesus himself may have taken symbolically some of the Old Testament statements about the work of the messiah. In general, when verbal statements are taken as symbolically true, this implies regarding them as presenting realities.

From symbolic truth we may pass on to *poetic truth*. There is much poetry in the Psalms and in the prophetic books. God is spoken of as sheltering people under his wings, as if he were a great bird with its chickens, or as a shepherd leading his sheep (the believers) into green pastures. A psalmist (19.5, 6) speaks of the sun as a bridegroom coming out of his chamber, or as a strong man running a race from one end of heaven to the other; and for those who believed that the sun went round the earth this is a way of expressing the fact. Poetic truth is a kind of extension of the usage of words in a secondary sense.

Somewhat similar to poetic truth is *pictorial truth*. The book of Jonah is an example of this. There was a prophet called Jonah (2 Kings 14.25), but the book of this name has nothing to do with the actual prophet, and is now generally regarded as a work of fiction. Yet it expresses one of the profoundest truths of the Old Testament, namely, the love of God for people other than the Jews, and, by implication, for all human beings.

The conception of pictorial truth is especially relevant to the infancy narratives in the first and third gospels. It is not generally recognized that these cannot both be literally true, since they contradict one another. According to Luke, Joseph and Mary arrived in Bethlehem from Nazareth on a day which we now identify as 24 December, and could only find lodging in a stable. Jesus was born during the ensuing night. They then remained in Bethlehem, presumably not all the time in the stable, until the fortieth day (2 February) in order to go to the Temple in Jerusalem for Mary's purification and the presentation of Jesus to God. After these events they returned to Nazareth. There is no place here for a visit to Egypt. If Luke is accepted there can be no factual truth in Matthew's narrative.

Matthew, if taken by himself, presents Joseph and Mary as residents in Bethlehem with a house (*oikia* – 2.11) of their own, in which the wise men visit them. On their return from Egypt their first thought was to go back to Bethlehem, but when they realized that Bethlehem was in the tetrarchy of Archelaus, a son of Herod the Great, they decided to move elsewhere. Eventually, but not immediately, they settled in Nazareth. The assertion that

Herod had all the boys of two years or less put to death suggests that the visit of the wise men was supposed to take place when Jesus was several months old.

There may be some factual truth in Luke's narrative, but it seems unlikely that, for the purpose of a census, the Romans would make large numbers of people go back to some place where they had formerly lived. What can be said about both narratives, however, is that they are presenting something of the significance of Jesus, and that this is something real. Siting the birth in Bethlehem supported the claim to messiahship, and Luke also shows other aspects of this. Matthew shows that the message of Jesus was for non-Jews as well as Jews, and that it would be opposed by some sections of the Jewish people.

Both narratives record the virginal conception of Jesus. Many Christians seem to think of this as a proof of his divinity, since it is easier to think of him as 'son of God' if he has no human father. What such Christians fail to realize is that nearly a thousand million Muslims accept the virgin birth (which is asserted in the Qur'an) but deny the divinity. For them the virginal conception is a miracle comparable to the birth of John the Baptist when his mother was a very old woman. Critics of Christian belief deny the factuality of the virginal conception on the grounds that there are no authenticated cases of this in the human race, although it is said to occur in some animal species. This last would make it conceivable that the visit of the angel so affected Mary that it caused a child to develop in her womb. On the whole it seems unlikely that this is what happened. That means that the story of the virginal conception and birth must be regarded as a pictorial presentation of the significance of Jesus, and as implying that from the moment of his conception he was being prepared for the task he ultimately fulfilled.

When we try to give an account of the achievements of Jesus we have to use pictorial language. To say that he redeemed the world implies that he did something like buying it back from slavery, and that is pictorial language rather than metaphorical. So is it to say that he saved the world, or that he reconciled humanity with God, or that he inaugurated a new covenant. These are pictorial statements, but at the same time they are a way of expressing profound truths.

What above all needs to be emphasized is that all these different kinds of truth are presentations of some of the basic and ultimate realities of this world in which we live.

Because of the limitations of our minds and because of the nature of these realities we cannot have the straightforward presentation of them that we would like. Yet what is presented is real; and some of the realities presented by poetic and pictorial truth, such as the incarnation of Jesus, are of the utmost importance for our lives. Moreover, despite our intellectual limitations we have sufficient knowledge of the basic realities to allow us to lead wholly meaningful lives.

GOD AND THE UNIVERSE   THREE

At the centre of the Christian religion is belief in God, but before considering this in detail it is well to remind ourselves that the human mind is incapable of obtaining a full knowledge of God. Much of what Christians know about God comes from specific divine revelations through prophets and other inspired persons. Apart from such revelations the human mind is capable of gaining some knowledge of God through its own efforts in what is known as rational or natural theology.

The limitation of our human knowledge of God is expressed pictorially in the Old Testament in a story about Moses (Exodus 33.18–23). Moses asked to see God's glory, but was told that no man could see God's glory and live. He was then put in a cleft in a rock and covered by God's hand; when God had passed, the hand was withdrawn, so that Moses could see the back parts. In other words there are limitations to what human beings can know of God. The basic truth of this picture-story is not brought into question by the fact that there are many other verses in the Old Testament which speak of people seeing God's face . . . Indeed earlier in the same chapter (verse 11) it is said that 'the Lord spoke to Moses face to face as a man speaks to his friend'.

In such passages the face of God must mean such knowledge of God as is possible for human beings.

Another aspect of the inadequacies of our knowledge of God is that we have no single image which stands for his reality. We may think of him as an old man, as a father, as a shepherd, and in other ways; but these words only tell us that God is something like the primary meaning of the words.

The Nicene Creed speaks of 'one God, the Father Almighty, maker of heaven and earth, and of all things visible and invisible'. This ties in with the account of creation at the beginning of the Bible (Genesis 1), where God is said to create all that exists in six days and to rest on the seventh day. Some Christians may take this to mean that after God had created the world he left it to carry on by itself in accordance with the powers he had formed in it. Such Christians fail to realize that the Bible presents God as continuously active in the world, sometimes interfering with natural processes, and in particular creating each individual human being. God's resting on the seventh day is a pictorial way of justifying the Jewish practice of doing no work on the sabbath or seventh day of the week. By presenting creation as extending over time and not as a single act this account comes closer to the scientific conception of the cosmic process, though the details do not correspond exactly.

Some of these points may be elaborated. God's creation of each human individual is illustrated by Job's statement: 'Your hands have made me and fashioned me' (10.8; and the same words are found in Psalm 119.73). Jeremiah (1.5) speaks of God 'forming him in the womb'. Another aspect of God's activity was speaking to prophets, that is, making revelations to them. Again it was generally believed by the Old Testament writers that God protected the Hebrew people, both by strengthening them and in other ways. Among the latter might be interfering with natural processes, as when he caused the sun and moon to stand still for Joshua, or brought about the plagues on the Egyptians which led to the exodus. Haggai (chapter 1) says that God has inflicted a severe drought on the returned exiles because, while building fine houses for themselves, they have failed to rebuild his temple. While modern Christians cannot accept the belief in God's interference with natural processes, they can see that God continues in many ways to act in human lives.

The failure of some Christians to believe in God's continuing activity in the world may also be due in part to the use by theologians of rational arguments to prove the existence of God, especially the so-called cosmological argument. This starts with the conception of God as an omnipotent, omniscient creator and then tries to prove by philosophical arguments that he exists. Even if the arguments are accepted as sound, all they prove is a Great First Cause, not the loving God of the Christian faith, and not the God who is continually active in human lives.

Our modern mentality prefers scientific methods of argument. This means that we start by looking at the nature of the world, and then consider how it has come to be what it is, and how it is controlled. For us the starting-point should be that this is a wonderful world for human beings to live in. It makes it possible for billions of us to lead a meaningful life. There are indeed natural disasters which inflict suffering, but the suffering so caused is far less than the suffering caused by other human beings, and people are gradually learning to cope with these natural disasters or to avoid them. Thus for vast numbers of people it is a wonderful world.

The Old Testament writers were aware of the wonderful character of the world. The author of Psalm 104, for example, praises God for all the wonders of creation. He has given us a solid earth and covered much of it with the sea. In the hills there are springs to give drink to animals, and trees where the birds can build their nests. He makes grass to grow for cattle to feed on, and other plants to give human beings their food and wine to cheer their hearts. The moon marks the seasons, and day and night enable human beings to alternate work and repose. The psalmist concludes: 'O Lord, how manifold are your works; in wisdom you have made them all; the earth is full of your riches;' and he then goes on to mention the sea as a place for living creatures and for ships.

There is also something very wonderful about life in all its forms, especially in human beings. It is amazing how millions of people can live and work together with a degree of harmony. It is amazing how much knowledge of various kinds is stored in a human mind. It is amazing how many inventions have been made for our comfort and convenience. Apart from the good things mentioned by the psalmist there are the forms of power of which human beings make use – coal, gas, oil, steam, electricity. These are all included in our world.

When we look at the world in this way, and then ask what power or powers have produced it and probably continue to control it, it seems clear that there must be 'something like' a loving and intelligent human will and purpose. It seems impossible, when one looks impartially at our wonderful world and at the wonders of human nature, to hold, as some unbelievers have maintained, that it is the result of 'a fortuitous concourse of atoms'. All this cannot have come into existence by mere chance. In response to this assertion, however, those who hold the world to have come about fortuitously will argue that, while to begin with the cosmic process went on fortuitously, once life appeared the life in plants and animals gave direction to the process and helped to bring about this wonderful world.

This is certainly an important point which needs to be looked at carefully. Is there in life something like an intelligent purpose?

The higher animals show such a purpose, and we may allow that there is something similar in lower forms of life. This purpose is subordinate to the two main drives in all plants and animals, namely, the drive to maintain the individual life and the drive to maintain the species. We may also allow that the working of these drives is able to produce many of the features which make the world such a wonderful place to live in.

There is one aspect of the evolutionary process, however, which these drives do not fully explain, namely, that in the process there is an upward movement towards what are usually allowed to be higher forms of life. As time goes on, plants and animals of greater complexity make their appearance; and this complexity means not only more elaborate physical bodies, but in the case of the higher animals the development also of greater intelligence and greater consciousness.

The Darwinian explanation of higher forms of life was that, when plants and animals reproduce themselves, there are sometimes slight mutations which are repeated in the following generations. Some mutations prove more successful in the struggle for existence, and in course of time replace the originals from which they developed. For long this view was accepted by scientists as accounting for the upward movement seen in evolution. Now, however, some are questioning it on the ground that chance mutations would be insufficient to account for the large steps upward that have occurred. In other words there must be something present in plants and animals which produces large upward-moving mutations. These could not have come about by a mere concourse of atoms. There must be an upward-moving power of some sort present in all life.

While atheists may think that the concept of life is itself a sufficient cause for the upward evolutionary movement, believers in God will take the view that his creative power must somehow be behind it; that is, that this power must somehow be present in life, even if there was nothing similar in pre-life. How life came to exist in the cosmic process may be a mystery we shall never be able to solve. A possible explanation, however, has been suggested by Pierre Teilhard de Chardin, a Christian thinker who was also a skilled palaeontologist and well versed in other sciences. After claiming that there was in life a factor making for greater complexity and greater consciousness, he went on to suggest that this factor was also present in pre-life, and in due course led to the appearance of life. This is a somewhat vague theory and not verifiable, but it is a possible explanation of the facts. If it is not accepted, the appearance of life remains an insoluble mystery. The decision on this point, however, does not really affect the Christian faith.

The matter is different, however, when we come to consider the upward movement in the evolutionary process in both animals and plants. Here the suggestion that there is in all life a factor making for greater complexity and greater consciousness seems a good way of explaining how mutations occurred of such a kind that their success in the struggle for existence led to higher species, and eventually to the appearance of human beings. Such an upward-moving factor, of course, is not yet a conception of God, but it may be seen as the method by which 'something like' a human intelligence and purpose controls the evolutionary process. The believer in God then sees God as working through this factor. Another way of expressing this would be to say that God is working through the life that is in plants and animals. This life might then be taken to be somehow derived from God's life. It is not God's life in its fullness, but through this created life God is active in our world. God may thus be said to be immanent in the world of living things, while at the same time being transcendent.

It must also be emphasized, of course, that God's activity in living things proceeds in a regular way, and that there are no acts of interference with natural processes as most Old Testament writers supposed. The life in plants and animals follows regular patterns. Where upward mutations occur, they come about in what might be called a natural way, as part of the normal working of each species.

Christian belief in God also sees him as having in some sense ultimate control of pre-life, but not as interfering in specific events. Science has now made it clear that everything in the material universe acts according to fixed unchanging laws. The believer sees these as having been established by God and as being maintained by him. It is obviously important for human beings to have a fixed order of things on which they can rely. Life would be extremely difficult without the fixity of the natural world – the rising and setting of the sun, the unchanging character of the many natural substances we use, and also the regular behaviour of plants and animals.

It is also helpful to consider belief in God by starting from the question 'What do we mean by reality, and what things do we regard as real?' In answering this question what occurs to us first are the visible material objects by which we are surrounded – the ground under us, our bodies and those of other people, the objects of which we make use, our houses, our food, and so on. All these are certainly real. We are forced to admit, however, that there are also invisible realities. We feel the wind blowing but cannot see it, although we can see its effect on objects such as trees; and scientists tell us that among the chemical elements which constitute the world there are invisible gases such as oxygen and nitrogen. Then there are the sounds and smells and tastes of which we are aware through the appropriate senses, and the heat and cold which we feel, although we cannot see any

17

of these. Another invisible reality with an important place in the world is electricity. We learn how to use it for our purposes, and how to avoid its dangers, and we see many of its effects, such as electric light; but electricity itself we cannot see.

Then there is the life which is in ourselves and in animals and plants. It is something like electricity, in that we see its effects and have little difficulty in distinguishing between living things and lifeless things; but life itself we cannot see. It has been maintained above that it is through life that God is working, and that it is a form of his creativity. Life might also be spoken of as an agent of God; but this is not a good metaphor, since the life in us may also be regarded as an aspect of God's own being.

It is easy to go on from these considerations to think of God as real, because he creates and sustains our lives and all the wonderful world in which we live; but there is no single image which adequately represents his being. We could think of him as an all-pervading power, something like electricity. At the same time, however, because there is in him 'something like' a human intelligence, will and purpose, it is appropriate to use images such as that of a father.

When people ask why a loving God permits so much suffering, the answer must be that this suffering does not come about through any direct action of God, but because he maintains the world as it is. In considering this question the suffering which comes to people from natural causes is to be distinguished from that which comes from other human beings, and will be dealt with first. Among these natural causes are earthquakes, volcanic eruptions, typhoons, tidal waves, floods and droughts. These are features of the world created by God, and they lead to the question why he should have created such a world, if he wanted it to be suitable for meaningful human life. The answer must clearly be that human beings, and also animals, require a world on which they can rely because it is stable and unchanging, that is, because all the material objects constituting the world obey fixed laws. We need to know that day and night will follow one another in a regular way, and that season will follow season. We need to know that water, fire, wood, metal and all the other elements we use will continue to function as they always have done, and likewise the plants and animals we use to feed ourselves and for other purposes. In short we need a world on which we can rely, and which makes it possible for us, as human life continues, to learn how to use it better and how for the most part to avoid the possible disasters. As we look at the vast extent of the human life which this reliable world makes possible, the sufferings from natural causes are relatively slight.

By far the largest part of human suffering comes from other human beings. All over the world at the present time there are wars and fighting which bring misery to millions. Even in settled and peaceful communities there are murderers, rapists, burglars, paedophiles and other criminals, who are bringing suffering to some of their fellow-citizens. When it is asked how it is that God could have created a world in which such things are possible, the answer must be that for a satisfactory life people must have freedom of will to the extent that they can make decisions which have consequences in the external world. Without such freedom there could be no truly human life; but this freedom means that individuals are capable of making decisions that bring suffering to others. To prevent the worst forms of causing suffering to others there have been set up in settled human communities methods of discouraging criminals, such as laws, law-courts and police forces, and in the world community bodies such as the United Nations and international courts of justice. Such arrangements may be seen as the outcome of inner promptings from God to individuals, even though he does not interfere directly against criminals, as most Old Testament writers realized. Sometimes wrongdoers may suffer from remorse of conscience, but there are many cases where this does not seem to happen.

If we keep these points in mind they give us a clear answer to the question why a loving God permits such suffering. We cannot have the wonderful world we have without there being the possibility of such suffering. The question is based on a false idea of God's omnipotence. That is taken to mean that God has the power to do absolutely anything he decides to do. From our observation of the world, however, we see that, even if God has such a power, he has decided not to use it. He does not interfere with the material world by suspending the operation of natural laws. In the case of human beings the matter is somewhat different, since God can act from within them, as it were. As, for example, when he calls a person to a particular task; but he certainly does not act from without by causing human decisions to have consequences other than those which come about naturally. This non-interference of God does not show a lack of love. Rather it shows that his love provides a wonderful world for human life, a world in which people can rely on natural events and substances, and on the effectiveness in general of their decisions.

Apart from suffering brought about by natural disasters, wild animals or other human beings, there are ways in which people can bring suffering on themselves. They can do so by faulty decisions or by such actions as losing control of a car. Again the doing of a wrongful act often leads to suffering of various kinds for the wrongdoer. A few will suffer from remorse of conscience, and many types of wrongdoing are punished by the state if the offender is caught. None of these forms of suffering raises any question about God's love.

There are also instances, though perhaps relatively few in number, where people feel that they are called by God to a specific task which they know may lead to suffering. The clearest examples of such people are the martyrs, who are prepared to go to their deaths in fulfilment of a God-given task. Outstanding here is the case of Jesus, who felt he was called to enter into a confrontation with his religious opponents, realizing, as he did, that it could lead to suffering and death. It would probably be wrong to say that God in his transcendence experiences suffering, even if we could understand what this meant; but it is clear that in the most perfect manifestation in human life of God's love there was an acceptance of suffering.

FOUR

GOD IN HUMAN LIFE   FOUR

While it is important for Christians to think of God as the reality which brought the universe into being and which continues to maintain it, it is even more important to have some understanding of the many ways in which God affects the life of human beings. Not only does he create all of them individually and maintain their existence, but he may also be active within each person in more spiritual ways.

The Creation of Human Beings

There has been a long tradition of regarding a human person as consisting of body and soul. The body was the physical part or aspect, and the soul the immaterial part or aspect, including consciousness, mind, feeling and the like. Many Greek philosophers held that the soul alone was the person, and that the body was only its instrument or habitation. Some went so far as to believe in the transmigration of souls, that is, that the same soul could inhabit different bodies at different times. Among Tibetan Buddhists today, when their leader, the Dalai Lama, dies, there is a search for the young boy in whom he has become reincarnated.

There have been forms of Christian belief in which it was held that the body was mortal and only the soul immortal. This meant that when a person died, the body disintegrated, while the soul went to heaven to be with God, at least if it fulfilled the necessary conditions. This is a dualistic conception of the human person, and modern thought now tends to reject such dualism. It may be possible for Christians to speak of body and soul without implying such dualism; but it is perhaps best to avoid the word 'soul' and to speak instead of the 'self'. One way of thinking of eternal life, too, is to regard human persons as being in the presence of God with the whole of their lives before them as it were in a moment of time; in this case the contribution of the body to the events of a person's life would have its place, even if the body itself no longer exists. Such a view of eternal life is probably better than thinking of it as an infinite continuation of this life in some kind of temporal setting. There are also Christians who look forward to 'everlasting rest' in the presence of God.

The human person or self, then, is a being living a physical life in this world, but at the same time having a consciousness of oneself or self-consciousness, something the animals probably do not have or at least not to the same extent. This consciousness includes mind or intelligence, will, feelings of various kinds and memory. Modern Christians should certainly accept the biblical assertion that God has individually created each human person, but they must then go on to consider how this is to be understood in detail.

It has been maintained above that God has controlled the evolutionary process by being in some way immanent in it. Human beings have their general characteristics as a result of the evolutionary process, and in this way may be said to have been formed by God. Individuals receive their more specific characteristics from parents, grandparents and other ancestors. Parents, of course, are only handing on the life they themselves received. We are so familiar with life in its various forms that we do not think much about it. Yet in some ways it is a great mystery. Perhaps we should see life as the agent of God through which he creates human beings. An agent, however, would be something separate from God, while the life in living things is more like an aspect of God's being, though it is not of course identical with the fullness of life which believers hold to exist in God himself.

All this links up with one of the profound insights of the Old Testament, namely, that God made human beings, men and women, in his own image (Genesis 1.27; 5.2). It follows from this that there is something humanlike in God; and so we think of God as having 'something like' a human mind, will and purpose, even if our conception of these is imperfect. At the same time it means that our human minds, wills and purposes are something like the analogues in God. To these the general feature of life must be added, so that the life which we experience in ourselves is 'something like' the fuller life of God. From this we might go on to hold that this life is in some sense God's immanence in us. It is through this life that he creates us, so he is active in it. To this extent we may speak of it as an aspect of God's being, but we also have to remember that, while God's life is full and perfect, there is much imperfection in our human life. This may be linked up with the freedom of our wills.

Human beings have been created with a certain will, which means that they are able to make choices and decisions which have an effect in the outside world. Choices and decisions, however, are not separate entities, but form a kind of hierarchy.

If I decide to go to a restaurant for a meal, I then have to make further choices of the items from the menu I want to receive. Some choices may cover great areas of one's life, such as the choice of a career or the choice of a marriage partner. Decisions to which other decisions or choices are subordinate may be called 'governing decisions'. Many choices, of course, are trivial, such as the choice whether or not to add marmalade to the toast one has already decided to eat and to eat buttered. In such simple choices, too, there is no explicit thinking; one just lifts a piece of toast and butters it.

In the religious life governing decisions are often taken. When individuals experience conversion, they may make a decision which will control the rest of their lives. They will decide that for the future they will serve God as they have come to understand his nature and how he ought to be served. Christians whose religion has, as it were, grown with them, and who have not experienced any sudden change of direction by conversion, may also at some time formulate their position as 'I will try at all times to do God's will', and they may repeat this annually or at other intervals. Something of this kind may also be included in every act of worship. When people feel they have received a special call from God, their positive response to it will be a governing decision.

That people have to make choices or decisions is a result of the general character of the nature with which they have been created. In this nature there are various drives, primarily the drive to maintain one's own life and the drive to maintain the race. These drives are shared with animals and plants. Human beings would also seem to have a drive to lead a meaningful life, since they are not usually satisfied with merely living, but want to feel that they have achieved something of value. Perhaps one should also recognize a drive to live in community, but in a sense this is involved in the drives to maintain one's own life and to maintain the race; yet a person undoubtedly gains much from being loved and appreciated by other persons. It is above all through the religious perspective that Christians find life meaningful. The farmer producing food is obviously doing something worthwhile, as is the person involved in manufacturing industry; but Christians want to see their activities as also having a place in the eternal purposes of God.

There are of course various ways in which our freedom of will is limited. Some of these come from the way in which our human nature is constituted. We cannot work continuously but have to stop for rest and/sleep. Our bodily movements are limited in various ways, and even the best athletes cannot run faster than about 15 miles an hour. We cannot go on indefinitely without food and drink. Our choices are also influenced by the emotional aspects of our natures. We have innate tendencies to react in certain ways to the situations in which we find ourselves and to some of the people we meet. Not all of our instinctive reactions are good. When one has been hurt by another person, there is a desire to get one's own back in some way, and, while this may sometimes be right, in most cases it will probably be wrong and will not contribute to a harmonious society, which is something we should be trying to bring about. Human sexuality makes an important contribution to maintaining the race, while at the same time creating many problems, but these need not be considered here. The moral law contained in the last six of the Ten Commandments – respect for property, respect for marriage, respect for life, truthfulness in public statements, honouring parents and absence of greed – is the necessary foundation of a harmonious community. It is not something arbitrary, but arises out of the way in which human nature has been constituted.

Our freedom of will is also restricted by our relations to other people. In the old days there were slaves who had to do what their owners wanted them to do. Nowadays a great many people are employed in various ways, such as manufacturing industry and in the distribution of goods, and these people have to do what their employers pay them to do. In entering employment, of course, people are making a choice. Sometimes a group of people come together to promote a cause in which they are interested and then appoint a leader over them; and they are then expected to follow the decisions of the leader.

There are also more material ways in which people fail to get what they have chosen. A group may arrange to go for a picnic on a particular day, and then find that on that day it is raining heavily. They can, of course, guard against disappointment by saying 'weather permitting'. People can also be mistaken about the nature of the material they are dealing with; a trivial example would be starting to spread butter on soft bread and finding the butter too hard to spread because it had been frozen. People can also be mistaken about more important matters. Those who think they can achieve a satisfactory and meaningful life by surrounding themselves with worldly comforts and luxuries will probably end up by finding their lives not very meaningful. In the case of basic or fundamental choices about the form of one's life it is important that these should be founded on true religious belief about the realities of our world.

Human freedom may also be said to be limited by the unconscious. I may do something for what I think is a particular reason, and then later on realize that there was also another and more important reason of which I was not aware at the time. There may also be occasions when people act from motives of which they are completely unconscious and remain unconscious, and it is only other people who are aware of these underlying motives. Although this is in a sense a limitation of human freedom, we still tend to say that unconsciously motivated people are acting freely; they are still making decisions, and these are having an effect on the world around them.

God's Special Activities within Human Lives

Besides creating human beings, God acts in human lives in various ways, as it were from within. There is abundant evidence for this in the Old and New Testaments and in the later experience of the Christian church; but there is no reason to deny that it also happens to believers in other religions. Christians sometimes speak of such matters as the work of the Holy Spirit or of the indwelling Christ. This divine activity may be brought under the following heads: *calling and guiding* people; *strengthening and supporting* people; *revealing* something of his nature and his will; giving believers an *awareness* of his presence. These matters will now be looked at in detail.

God calls and guides people

There are many Christians who believe that God is calling them to do a particular piece of work. Often this is some work of a religious kind, such as becoming a priest or monk or nun; but it may also be something less obviously religious, such as going to cheer a lonely neighbour, or giving a helping hand to someone in difficulties. There are various ways in which people experience the call to a particular task. Some may hear a voice. Some, without hearing a voice, may become convinced that God is wanting them to do something. Others, while believing that as Christians they must set about a particular piece of work, do not think of this explicitly as a direct call from God. There are also other possibilities. Elsewhere I have suggested 'inner promptings' as a general term for all the different ways in which people come to feel they ought to be doing a piece of work. In the Old Testament these promptings are sometimes given an external form, as when Moses is said to have seen a burning bush.

There are many examples in the Bible of people receiving such calls. Abraham was called to leave the land in which he was living and go westward in the direction of Palestine (Genesis 31.3). Moses, while in Midian, had a vision by which he felt called to go back to Egypt to deliver his fellow Hebrews from the servitude and genocide they were experiencing there (Exodus 3.1–10). Through his being anointed by Samuel, David may be said to have had a call to work for the establishment of a kingdom in which the Hebrew tribes would be united and secure (1 Samuel 16.13). The later prophets, whose books we have, thought they were called by God to bring their fellow citizens back to the true worship of God and complete obedience to his laws. In the New Testament the twelve apostles were called on to follow Jesus and then to proclaim his gospel to the world, while the outstanding experience of a call is that which changed Saul/Paul from a persecutor of the church to its principal missionary to the gentiles. It was also felt, especially in New Testament times, that when people set about carrying out the task to which they had been called by God, he continued to show them the details of what he wanted done, and so was guiding them.

While some people may receive a call from God without recognizing it as such, others may think they have received a call when that is not the case. In the Old Testament there were those labelled as 'false prophets' by the writers, who were mistaken about what they claimed was a revelation from God, as, for example, when they told a king he would be victorious, and then later in the battle he was defeated and sometimes killed. In modern times supposed revelations from God have led to the formation of far-out sects and other aberrations from mainstream Christianity.

Probably the best way of distinguishing whether inner promptings come from God or not is by applying the criterion of fruits – 'by their fruits you shall know them' (e.g. Matthew 7.16). An inner prompting may be said to have good fruits when what results from it is some betterment in the life of the community or of the individual, and then it may be held to come from God. On the other hand, when following a prompting leads to some deterioration in the life of the community or of the individual, it is clear that the prompting has not come from God but is the outcome of instinctive forces in the person receiving it. When Christians receive some inner prompting which they think relayed from God, they should try to assess it by looking at its possible fruits if carried out. Even something which looks as if it might be good for themselves may be bad for the community. The same test, of course, should be applied to inner promptings which are not thought of as coming from God. It will sometimes happen too that when people look back on their lives and see the good that has resulted from following some prompting, they will feel that it must have come from God although they were not aware of this at the time; and they will then realize that in this way God was leading and guiding them.

God strengthens and supports people

There is a widespread belief among Christians that as they go about trying to do God's will and lead a Christian life, they are given the power to do this from a divine source; and they mostly think of this power as the Holy Spirit. As Moses continued to lead the people from Egypt through the wilderness for forty years, he must have felt that God was supporting him. There are numerous references in the Psalms to people being given the power to fight and be victorious. One psalmist speaks of God girding him with strength of war or strength of battle, and teaching his hands to fight (18.32, 34, 39) Another speaks of God as his strength, who teaches his hands to war and his fingers to fight (144.1). The receiving of such strength was particularly important in these ancient times when fighting was hand to hand.

The strength that comes from God is also important for those who go about God-given tasks and meet with difficulties and opposition. The apostle Paul was aware of receiving such strength as he went about his missionary activity and encountered hostility, and he usually thought of this strength as coming from the Holy Spirit. It is clearly important for modern Christians to know that God is active in human lives in this way, and that he is always present and ready to help if they know how to accept what he offers. God can help us to perform the tasks he has given us, and also to lead a better life in general.

God's revelation of himself

Where there is some true knowledge of God's nature and of his will, as there is in Christianity, and probably also in the other great religions, this should be seen as coming from God by way of his revealing something of himself. The Old Testament prophets thought they heard God speaking to them and giving them messages they were to hand on to their fellow citizens. It is perhaps mainly because of the experience of these prophets that we speak of God's revelation of himself to human beings.

This may also come in other ways, however. Christians believe that they learn something of the love of God from the mission and teaching of Jesus and above all from the climax of that mission; and some Christians would say that this was taught to them by God the Holy Spirit, although they did not hear any words. Thus knowledge of God can come to people in many different ways, but all of these are to be ascribed to God's own activity. The knowledge of God, of course, does not come all at once, but is learnt gradually over centuries in a believing community which tries to live according to what it has already learnt about God. Within such a community a few individuals from time to time receive further revelations developing or correcting or improving what is already known.

In recent centuries probably few Christians have had such intense experiences as the Hebrew prophets. One might perhaps allow that Luther, for instance, had had revelations which led to the correction of faults in the contemporary church. Many ordinary Christians, however, come at some point to have a deeper appreciation of aspects of God's being, and this may be seen as due to his activity. Indeed, something of this kind perhaps happens to everyone. To begin with all of us are taught the Christian faith by other persons, but, as we continue in communion with the church and progress in the Christian life, we usually come to a deeper appreciation of the truths about God; and this should be seen as coming from his activity in us. It is also a fact, of course, that some Christians think they are receiving divine revelations of a sort, although to impartial observers this seems to be no more than something from their own imagination.

Believers can have some awareness of God's presence with them

In today's world there are many Christians who claim that occasionally or perhaps frequently they have an experience of God's presence with them. This experience might come to them in a church or temple or other sacred place. Different persons will describe the experience in very different ways, and the sceptic will say it is all imagination. Yet the alleged experience is so widespread, and in many instances seeming to lead to an improvement in the quality of the person's life, that it cannot be dismissed as mere imagination, There is a reality in it, and this must be ascribed to the working of God. The vagueness in some of the descriptions may be blamed on the limitations of the human mind.

At this point I might mention a personal experience. Some years ago I selected as a basis for meditation the words of a psalm (73.24): 'whom have I in heaven but thee; and there is none upon earth I desire in comparison of thee'; and to these I added 'my ever-loving Lord and my God'. Now in quiet moments I frequently find these words thrusting themselves into my consciousness, sometimes more than once a day. I do not regard this as an awareness of God; yet there is a sense in which God is here coming into my life.

The Old Testament writers were not good at describing what we now regard as inner experiences, but had to give them an external visible and material form. Thus when Moses received the call from God to go back to Egypt and work for the deliverance of his people, he is said to have seen a bush burning without being consumed, and to have heard a voice coming from it (Exodus 3.2–10). Even in the New Testament in the account of the temptations of Jesus the tempter is said to have taken him to a pinnacle of the temple and then to a high mountain from which he could see all the kingdoms of the world; but we should regard these as descriptions of inner experiences.

As further examples of experiencing God's presence two incidents in the life of Jacob may be looked at. The first was when his mother sent him from Palestine to her relatives in Iraq to remove him from possible maltreatment by his brother Esau. As he slept in the open he had a vision of angels ascending and descending a ladder from heaven and bringing him a message of encouragement. When he woke he said, 'Surely God is in this place, and I did not know it' (Genesis 28.16). The second incident occurred years later when Jacob was bringing his family, his possessions and his livestock back to Palestine, and was afraid that Esau might attack them. He sent presents ahead to propitiate Esau, but when he came to the ford at Jabbok new fears assailed him, since once he had crossed it there would be no way of avoiding a confrontation with Esau. At the ford Jacob spent a whole night wrestling with a man. This is presumably the externalized description of an inner experience. The struggle was between his fear of Esau and his desire to have a good future for his family. The man he wrestled with was presumably urging him to take the risk of going on, and he eventually decided to do so. As he later reflected on the matter, he called the place Peniel, for he said, 'I have seen God face to face and my life is preserved' (Genesis 32.22).

GOD IN THE OLD TESTAMENT FIVE

General Considerations

A traditional view of the Old Testament was that it had all
been directly revealed by God, and that every word in it was true.
For a number of reasons, some of which will be discussed here,
such a view is impossible for the modern Christian. The Old
Testament is, of course, a basic document for the Christian faith,
and has many passages showing deep insight into the nature
of God and of his dealings with humanity. Essentially, however,
it is a record of how belief in God developed in the people who
eventually became the Jews. It is the picture of a developing
religion. As a religion develops, too, some of the earlier stages
have to be completely abandoned. This certainly applies to the
Old Testament, but many Christians may not appreciate the fact
because they read only selected passages.

The most serious criticism of the Old Testament is that some
of it is definitely un-Christian. This was recognized by the bishops
of the Scottish Episcopal Church when they produced a new
prayer book in 1929. They put brackets round some of the verses
of the Psalms to indicate that they might be omitted in public

worship because of the un-Christian character of the assertions. In one of the worst of these passages it is said that the man is blessed who takes the babes of Israel's enemies and dashes them against a rock (137.7–10). Apart from the Psalms, however, there are many other un-Christian elements in the Old Testament. Moses ordered a man to be stoned to death for what seems to us the petty sin of 'working' on the sabbath by collecting a few sticks to make a fire (Numbers 15.32–6); presumably it was felt that this was endangering the relationship of the whole community to God. Again, when Joshua conquered Jericho he was told to put every living thing in it to death – men, women, children and animals; and something similar was done at Ai. These actions took place in accordance with commands from God.

The extermination of whole populations, as at Jericho, was more extensive than appears from a casual reading of the Authorized Version and some other translations. The basic Hebrew word is *herem*, which is usually translated 'destroy utterly' or 'utterly destroyed' in the Authorized Version; but in the verse about Jericho (Joshua 6.17) it is said that 'the city shall be accursed, even it and all that are in it', while in the margin it is suggested that 'accursed' might be replaced by 'devoted'. The Jerusalem Bible normally uses the phrase 'the curse of destruction', and this gives a better idea of what was happening. The whole was essentially a religious act. Either because he had received a command from God, or because he had made a vow in order to secure God's favour, a military commander 'devoted' the whole of an enemy town to God, perhaps as a kind of sacrifice. In practice this meant the slaughter of all the men, women and children, and sometimes also of the animals. At Jericho the material possessions of the inhabitants were also included, apart from the precious metals. On the other hand, when the people of Jabesh were thus put under the curse of destruction, the girls who were still virgin were excepted (Judges 21.8–14). During the period of settlement Jericho, Ai and a number of other towns were thus devoted to God and the inhabitants killed (Joshua 6.21; 8.26; 19.28–40; 11.11f.; Judges 1.17). Earlier, east of Jordan, the same treatment had been meted out to the kings Sihon and Og and their peoples (Deuteronomy 3.6); and later Samuel commanded Saul to do the same to Agag and his people (1 Samuel 15.3, 8f., 15–20). Such are the assertions of the Old Testament writers. It is possible that they exaggerated the extent to which this policy of 'devotion to God' was followed, and it is also possible that many were able to escape from the general massacre; but, even so, there seems to have been a horrendous amount of slaughter.

Against this background modern Christians will want to consider the question whether the God and Father of our Lord Jesus Christ could have given such commands. Many will be inclined to answer, No; but this would be wrong, for it would imply abandoning the Old Testament, which is an essential part of our Christian faith. The solution of this difficulty is to recognize that the Old Testament is an account – not always in accordance with considerations of historical objectivity – of how knowledge of God grew and developed among the Hebrew tribes and the later Jews. There is development in many human affairs, and where this occurs some aspects of the earlier stages may have to be abandoned. The commands that God gives are primarily commands appropriate to the contemporary situation of the recipients. In some cases, but not in all, they may have a more permanent relevance. We should allow that the commands to devote whole communities to destruction were appropriate to the conditions in which the Hebrew tribes then found themselves. The times were hard and a degree of military power was necessary for a community to survive. A community which was able to exterminate the whole of another community would be greatly feared and respected. It is doubtful, however, whether the military superiority of the Hebrew tribes was so great as is suggested in the book of Joshua. It was only under Kings Saul and David that they became the dominant power in Palestine. In the time of Joshua fighting to maintain oneself against enemies was essential, and in this way the command of God was probably appropriate.

The account of Jephthah, one of the 'judges', contains material which shows how for long Hebrew religion retained beliefs that were eventually abandoned. When some of the Hebrew tribes were being threatened by the Ammonites, they prevailed on Jephthah to be their leader. Jephthah defended the right of the Hebrews to occupy the territories the Ammonites were trying to seize, and he said to the latter that these territories had been given to the Hebrews by Yahweh their God, and that the Ammonites should be content with what had been given to them by their god Chemosh (Judges 11.24). Jephthah presumably worshipped only Yahweh, but he believed that other gods existed and had some powers; and this shows that he had not yet reached the later Jewish belief in Yahweh as God alone. Later, when he returned victorious, he was led, because of a vow he had made, to offer up his only child, a daughter, as a sacrifice (Judges 12). If a prominent person like Jephthah held such views, many ordinary Hebrews of the time must have thought similarly. This marks an early stage of Old Testament religion which had clearly been abandoned by the later prophets and their followers, although some of the psalmists still spoke of Yahweh as being greater than other gods (Psalms 95.3; 97.9;135.5).

It is next necessary to realize that the Old Testament writers had nothing like our sense of historical objectivity. Some were editors rewriting existing books, and in doing so they did not hesitate to make alterations so that the picture of some past events was what they thought appropriate for their contemporaries. That the account of Jephthah has survived is probably due to the fact that some of these writers wanted to preserve all the material that came into their hands. This feature has some curious results. When a writer found two different accounts of some past event, he did not try to decide which was true, but produced a conflation in which something of each was retained. A clear example of this is the account of how Joseph was sent to Egypt by his brothers (Genesis 37.12–30). According to one version, when the brothers had seized Joseph and were about to kill him, Reuben persuaded them not to take any active steps but to leave him at the bottom of a dry well. Reuben presumably hoped to rescue him later. When the brothers were some distance away, however, a passing caravan of Midianites found Joseph, took him to Egypt and sold him there as a slave. When Reuben went back and found the well empty, he was greatly distressed. The other version is that it was Judah who persuaded the brothers not to kill Joseph, but instead to sell him for twenty shekels to a caravan of Ishmaelites who happened to pass; and it was these who sold him in Egypt. In our text the two versions are fused into one. The first version is found in verses 21–5, 28a, 29–30 and 36; The second occurs in verses 25–7 and 28b.

There is a somewhat similar conflation of two stories of how some men wanted to replace Aaron (Numbers 16). One lot was Korah and his party, and the others were Dathan, Abiram and their followers. The two groups suffered different fates; the earth opened beneath Korah's party and their families and swallowed them; but the others were destroyed by fire from heaven as they tried to offer incense.

The books of Joshua and Judges are a more elaborate example of contradictory accounts being retained. The book of Joshua gives the impression that by the time Joshua died all the Hebrew tribes had been securely settled in the territories assigned to them. The book of Judges, however, shows that this was far from being the case, and that many of them were still at the mercy of stronger neighbours. They only became dominant in Palestine as a result of the efforts of Saul and David.

False Assumptions of Old Testament Writers

Many of the Old Testament writers base their accounts of the past on assumptions which cannot be accepted by modern Christians. It is important to identify these:

God is able to interfere with natural processes

Many Old Testament writers had a belief in God's omnipotence according to which he was able to interfere with natural processes, whereas modern Christians accept the scientific view that natural events occur according to fixed laws. A very obvious example of this assumption, which was mentioned above, is the account in the book of Joshua (10.12–15) of how God caused the sun and the moon to stand still in the sky for the better part of a day, and this enabled Joshua and his men to gain a resounding victory over their opponents.

Another alleged event which could not possibly have happened is the flood from which Noah escaped (Genesis 6–8). It is obviously impossible that there should have been a flood covering Mount Ararat and that the water should then somehow have been reduced to sea level. Even a flood covering the much lower hills of Palestine would have been impossible. The story was presumably developed from conditions in Iraq. In that country there are vast stretches of low-lying flat land, and floods occur which cover large areas, even if the water is not more than a few metres deep. The biblical account exaggerates greatly the extent of the flood, but the story should be accepted as a pictorial presentation of important truths.

In the Psalms and elsewhere God is thought of as interfering with natural processes in order to punish people for sinful conduct. This belief is found as late as the prophet Haggai (1.1–11), who asserted that God had caused a drought to punish the exiles who had returned to Jerusalem and who had built fine houses for themselves but had not rebuilt God's temple.

The plagues in Egypt which enabled the Hebrews to make their escape from servitude and genocide were likewise said to have been brought about by God specially for this purpose. All of them, however, except the last (the death of the first-born) are natural events, though more severe than usual, and the modern believer has no reason to think that God interfered to bring them about. Moses, indeed, may have believed that God had brought them about specially, and may have persuaded Pharaoh that this was so.

God is able to intervene from without in human affairs

The modern Christian certainly believes that God intervenes in human affairs, as was shown in the last chapter. God does this by calling people to particular tasks, guiding them as they go about these, strengthening them if they meet with difficulties, and so on. All this is God working in human lives, as it were from within. At certain points, however, Old Testament writers thought of God as acting on human beings in other ways, which can be described as from without; and it is this which must be held to be mistaken.

As examples of such intervention from without we may take certain prophetic assertions with regard to the destruction of the kingdoms of Israel and Judah by the Assyrians and Babylonians. Amos (6.14) says, 'I [God] will raise a nation against you'; and Jeremiah (5.15) says, 'I will bring a nation against you.' There was no need for God to take any specific action in these cases. The Assyrians and Babylonians were military empires which in their heyday extended their rule over all the neighbouring peoples. They did not need to be prodded from without, as it were, to subdue the two kingdoms. Somewhat different is the assertion of Isaiah (44.28; 45.1) that Cyrus had been anointed by God to restore the exiles to Jerusalem. Cyrus had a belief in God, perhaps not very different from that of the Hebrews, and might have received inner promptings from God. He was also head of an empire, however, and as such believed in getting the support of local religious groups; and it was for this reason that he encouraged the exiles to return to Jerusalem. There is no need to suppose that God somehow imposed this on him from without.

When the Old Testament writers speak of God interfering with human activity from without or interfering with natural processes, they often say that this is an expression of his anger. He is angry with the wicked, with the enemies of his chosen people and with the worshippers of idols; and in his anger he desires to punish such people. How are such assertions to be reconciled with the Christian conception of God as a God of love?

Because there is something humanlike in God it is not inappropriate to speak of his anger. It is 'something like' human anger. Clearly God must disapprove in some way of those who go against his commands. This does not mean, however, that he takes specific actions against them. He has so constituted human society that it has developed forces for the maintenance of law and order and for the achievement of a harmonious community. Offenders are punished when caught, though some escape. God has also given human beings a conscience, and in some cases, though not in all, this punishes wrongdoers with a feeling of remorse. Beyond that, however, God does not seem to go.

According to Christian teaching God continues to love sinners and wrongdoers and hopes for their repentance. On one occasion some Jews brought before Jesus a woman who had been caught in the act of adultery and asked if she should be stoned in accordance with Mosaic law. Jesus replied that he who was without sin should cast the first stone. At this the accusers all melted away leaving Jesus and the woman alone. He asked, 'Where are your accusers?' and then added, 'Neither do I condemn you; go and sin no more' (John 8.3–11). This is the attitude which is at the centre of Christian teaching. By sinning people cut themselves off from God, and this may have permanent consequences unless they eventually repent; but God's love is such that repentance and reform of life is always open to them. Since this is the case, it would seem that God's anger can be given only a secondary and minor place in Christian teaching. Even some of the Old Testament writers insisted that God was 'slow to anger' (e.g. Nehemiah 9.17).

God fully protects upright persons

An important strand in Old Testament thought was that God gives complete protection to those who lead an upright life. One psalmist (37, esp. 23–6) asserts that 'I have been young and now am old, yet never have I seen the upright forsaken and his seed begging their bread.' Another psalmist (91.11, 12) said to the upright person, 'God has given his angels charge over you to guard you in all your ways; in their hands they will bear you up lest you dash your foot against a stone.' This belief was linked with the belief that God would fully support his chosen people so long as they obeyed his commands and did not worship idols.

It was also realized, however, that upright persons could be attacked by enemies and made to suffer in various ways. In such cases it seemed that, at least for the time being, God was not protecting them. Thus we have psalms where the psalmist is appealing to God for delivery from the suffering and persecution he is undergoing. One of the best known of these passages is the one Jesus quoted on the cross, from Psalm 22. Others are Psalms 35 and 71 (esp. 10–12). In these psalms there is nothing to justify the view that the suffering was due to sin; the sufferer is an innocent victim.

A further step was taken by Isaiah when he saw God's servant suffering as he went about the work assigned to him by God. This thought is contained in the fourth of the poems about the servant (Isaiah 52.13–53.12). Jesus was almost certainly aware of Isaiah's picture of the servant of God, and in the temptation to throw himself from the pinnacle of the temple (to be described in the next chapter) accepted the inevitability of suffering in the course of his mission.

A corollary of God's protection of the upright was his punishment of sinners. Yet the Old Testament writings show an awareness that in many cases the wicked seemed to flourish more than the upright. One psalmist (73.3–19) describes somewhat bitterly the prosperity of the ungodly, but in the end consoles himself with the thought that this prosperity is only for a time and that in the end it will disappear. Job (21.7–13) describes the prosperity of the wicked, but sees it as continuing until they die in peace.

Serious forms of suffering are due to sin

The belief that God protects the upright had as a kind of corollary the belief that great suffering is due to sin. In the book of Job the friends who came to comfort him insisted that his troubles must be due to some sin he had committed; but Job firmly denied this. The book of Job is thus a protest against what seems to have been the dominant belief.

Despite the existence of the book of Job the belief that great suffering was due to sin continued into New Testament times. On one occasion, when confronted by a man born blind, the disciples asked Jesus whether it was the man himself or his parents who had sinned (John 9.1–3). On another occasion he was told about some Galileans who had been killed by Pilate while carrying out sacrifices, and about some people in Siloam who had been killed by the collapse of a tower; and he was asked whether these had been greater sinners than their neighbours (Luke 13.1–5). In all these cases Jesus rejected the suggestion that the suffering was due to greater sin.

Even when no great suffering was involved an unfortunate occurrence could be said to be due to sin. Moses had led the tribes for forty years through the wilderness and brought them to the borders of the promised land, but his death before he actually entered it was alleged to be due to a slight sin he had committed much earlier (Deuteronomy 32.48–51). For the modern believer, however, there is no need to find a sin to explain this point, for Moses was advanced in years and death was natural. The death of King Saul in the battle of Mount Gilboa is treated as a punishment of his sin in disobeying Samuel (1 Samuel 15.10–35). Here, however, there are grounds for thinking that in his later years Saul's faith in God had declined. It is probably, too, because of his alleged sin that his great achievements as king and military leader receive only a brief mention (1 Samuel 14.47–8). Again, when many of the leading inhabitants of the two later kingdoms had been taken into exile, the prophets Jeremiah and Ezekiel told them that this was due to their sins; and this certainly helped the exiles to maintain faith in God and not to think that he had deserted them. It is doubtful, however, whether, even if they had avoided all sins, they could have escaped from the advances of the Assyrian and Babylonian empires.

Inadequate ideas about other religions

The Old Testament shows different attitudes to other religions at different periods. Moses may have believed that Yahweh, the deity he worshipped, was the creator of the universe and the only god. What was said about Jephthah, however, shows that for long many Hebrews believed that other gods existed and had certain powers. This seems to be reflected in various passages in the Psalms which speak of other gods; for example, where it is said that 'Yahweh is a great God and a great king above all gods' (95.3). Modern believers may take such passages as being expressed poetically, but the writers may have understood them literally and thus acknowledged the other gods in some sense.

When we come to the later prophets the situation has altered. One of the matters they had to deal with in their critique of their contemporaries was the acceptance of the gods of earlier inhabitants of Palestine, who had not been exterminated and with whom some of them had intermarried. These gods were mainly Baals and Astartes, whom we would now describe as fertility deities. This means that they represented human and animal sexuality, and that with their worship were associated practices contrary to the Mosaic law, such as sacred prostitution.

The prophets attacked such worship by pointing to the idols representing the deities and insisting on their impotence, their inability to hear, see or do anything. This may have been effective up to a point, but many of the worshippers may have been aware that the idols represented real powers. Modern Christians, with their knowledge of comparative religion, clearly cannot accept the prophets' view of the idols.

The Basic Truths of the Old Testament

While there is thus much in the Old Testament which modern Christians must regard as a mistaken understanding of historical events and of God's nature and will, there is also much deep spiritual and religious truth from which they have much to learn. It is worth emphasizing some aspects of this essential truth.

The humanlike aspect of God's being

Early in the book of Genesis (1.26–7; 5.2) it is stated that God made human beings, men and women, in his own image. This is a profound insight of great importance, for it implies that there is something humanlike in God. In other words the power which initiated the cosmic process and continues in some respects to control it has in it something like a human mind, will and purpose. Our images of God are all inadequate, but it helps to think of this humanlike quality.

This humanlike quality in God makes it easier for us to think about God, even though all the images we use are inadequate. The image of father – 'Our Father in heaven' – has been helpful, especially when Christians meet together to worship God; yet it can give no more than a slight suggestion of his great reality.

There is far more in God than a fatherlike quality. His creative activity has been compared to that of a potter making pots; but creativity is only part of his being. The divine working in human beings (to be described in the next section) is often ascribed to the Holy Spirit; but care must be taken not to use this image in such a way as to threaten the divine unity, since that is something which Christians must strongly affirm at the present time. Jesus is also in some sense an image of God, but this matter will be discussed in a later chapter. Whatever image we have before us when thinking about God, we have to realize that the being of God is much more extensive than is suggested by the image.

God is active in human beings in various ways

God's activity in human lives was described in the previous chapter, namely, how he calls people to specific tasks and guides them as they go about these, how he strengthens and supports them as they meet difficulties and opposition, how he reveals to them something of his nature and of his purposes for human life, and sometimes gives them a sense of his presence with them. In the psalms particularly and in the prophets there are many profound insights into these matters.

God called Abraham to lead to a higher form of religion

The Bible places Abraham at the beginning of the development of the specifically Hebrew and Jewish form of religion. It is assumed that Abraham worshipped God as later conceived, but we can have no precise knowledge of his belief. He certainly believed in and worshipped a deity, but he may have believed that other deities existed. Nevertheless we may allow that it was

God who was acting in Abraham in the two decisions we go on to consider, namely, the decision to leave Iraq, and the decision not to sacrifice his son Isaac but to regard a ram as a proper substitute.

The proposed sacrifice of Isaac may be looked at first (Genesis 22.1–19). The writer of Genesis says that God called on Abraham to sacrifice his son merely in order to test him, but not meaning him to carry it out. This, however, is contrary to the modern Christian conception of God. The probability is that Abraham inherited belief in a deity whose favour in a time of crisis could be secured by the sacrifice of a human being. In some great crisis about which we are not informed Abraham felt that in order to survive he would have to sacrifice Isaac, the son through whom alone he hoped to have descendants. He was obviously reluctant to do this, but felt it was necessary, and set about the actual sacrifice. When he saw a ram caught in a thicket, however, he took this as a sign from God that this would be a proper substitute. Human sacrifice then came to be forbidden in later Hebrew religion and in Judaism, but the Bible records numerous individuals making human sacrifices. In the time of the judges Jephthah still thought it permissible. In the later time of the two kingdoms, however, human sacrifice may have been due in part to the continuing influence of the pagan religions previously practised in Palestine.

The decision to leave Iraq was somewhat different (Genesis 12.1–5). Here it must be remembered that Abraham was not an individual with his own family but the head of a group of several hundred nomadic pastoralists (cf. Genesis 14.14). Much of Iraq is very flat country, and this had led to the development of arable farming based on irrigation. This in turn required a degree of centralized control such as was provided by the Accadian and Sumerian empires (prior to 2000 BCE). As irrigation spread there was less land for the pasturing of animals, and this was doubtless why Abraham's family had moved from southern to northern Iraq (Genesis 11.31). The continuing pressure on pastoralists even there doubtless had much to do with Abraham's decision to move westwards. Abraham was presumably aware of the religious dimension, however, and felt that he would be freer to worship God as he thought proper if he left Iraq. To this extent we can see the decision to leave Iraq as the response to a genuine call from God.

God brought about the exodus and the settlement in Palestine

Under Abraham's grandson Jacob the ancestors of the Hebrew tribes had settled in Egypt to avoid a famine. This had been possible because Jacob's son Joseph had been elevated to a position of authority there. The group continued to live in Egypt for over four hundred years and increased in number, though they were probably not so numerous as the Bible suggests. Eventually, however, the Egyptians reduced them to a kind of servitude and also began a form of genocide, namely, the killing of all male babies. Moses was a baby who escaped being killed, and had the good fortune to be adopted by an Egyptian princess and given the best of educations. Despite this he felt close to his fellow Hebrews, and when in protecting one he killed an Egyptian, he had to flee to Midian. After some years, however, he had a call from God (described in pictorial terms in the book of Exodus) bidding him return to Egypt and work for the deliverance of the Hebrews. This call from God is in a sense the beginning of the exodus.

When Moses appealed to the Egyptians to let his people go to conduct a sacrifice, they refused; and this was followed by the ten plagues. As has already been noted, nearly all of these were natural disasters, though perhaps more severe than usual; but they were alleged by the Bible to have been specially brought about by God. Moses seems to have persuaded Pharaoh that they were indeed from God, and in this way induced him to let the Hebrews leave. On the journey to the promised land the Bible alleges various miracles to have been brought about by God, to deliver the Hebrews from their enemies, to prevent them dying of thirst or starvation, and to overcome obstacles. Modern believers find natural explanations for the various events, so that they do not imply special intervention by God. God may, however, be seen as bringing the Hebrews to Palestine by the strength of character he gave to Moses, which enabled him to maintain control of the people he was leading, and to overcome the many difficulties they experienced as they moved through what was described as a wilderness. Doubtless, too, there were many with a firm belief in God who were able to give support to Moses. For these reasons modern Christians can see the success of the exodus as being due to the working of God.

Something similar may be said about God's responsibility for the final successful settlement in Palestine. As was pointed out above, this was much slower than is suggested in the book of Joshua, and was only completed by Kings Saul and David. What can be said is that, when the Hebrew tribes managed to settle in the promised land, this was due to the inner strength and courage they received from their belief in God. God must undoubtedly have given great inner strength to the various leaders. In these ancient times, when fighting was hand to hand, inner strength and courage were of great importance.

God sent the prophets

After the death of Solomon in 931 BCE, rivalries between leaders led to the division of the Hebrews into two kingdoms, known as the kingdoms of Israel and Judah; and these were sometimes at war with one another. Both kingdoms maintained the worship of God, whom they usually referred to as Yahweh (formerly transliterated Jehovah), though the northern kingdom had to develop shrines to replace Jerusalem, which was the capital of the southern kingdom. In both kingdoms some belief in the pagan deities of the previous inhabitants seems to have continued, perhaps especially in the northern one. There in the reign of Ahab (874–53) his wife Jezebel, who came from the Baal-worshipping family which ruled Sidon, tried to replace the worship of Yahweh with that of Baal. At this point God moved the prophet Elijah to resist this, and the proclamations of Elijah and of his follower and successor Elisha led to some revival of belief in Yahweh, and to the formation of a body of men who were able to defeat the Baal-worshippers and deprive them of positions of authority, though the worship of Baal was far from being completely eradicated.

Even after this, however, there were many in both kingdoms, from the kings downward, who did not follow all God's moral commands and did not maintain his worship in its purity. To deal with this situation God inspired a number of prophets, beginning with Amos (about the year 750) to recall people to a truer religion. The books of these prophets are preserved in the Old Testament. The prophets called the attention of the rulers and of their fellow citizens to the points at which they were failing to observe God's commands properly and falling short in their worship. This no doubt did something to maintain the religious life of the communities. The prophets also received deeper insight into the nature and character of God and of his relations with humanity. This led them to see God's choice of the Hebrew people not merely as something for their own benefit, but also that they might share their growing knowledge of him with other human beings, since these also had a place in his purposes.

A traditional view of the prophets was that they were primarily persons capable of foretelling the future, not critics of their own society; and certainly the prophets spoke of disasters ahead if people persisted in their wrong courses. The modern believer should realize that many of these prophecies of the future were not fulfilled in detail, if at all, even if some of them were; but this should not be taken as falsifying or belittling their critique of contemporary society.

God brought about the restoration from exile

The kingdom of Israel was conquered by the Assyrians in 722 or 721, and that of Judah by the Babylonians in 597 and again in 587 or 586. In both cases a large number of the inhabitants, including all the upper classes, were deported and resettled in Iraq, while, at least in the first case, people from other parts of the empire were settled in Palestine. In the sixth century the prophets Jeremiah and Ezekiel interpreted this exile as a punishment from God for their failure to keep all his commandments and to maintain a pure worship. This view was in accordance with the widely accepted belief that God intervened in human affairs in such ways, a belief which is not acceptable to modern Christians. The Assyrian and Babylonian empires were great military establishments eager to extend their power wherever possible. They needed no external prodding from God, as it were, to turn their attention to the Palestinian kingdoms. The most that can be said is that, if the southern kingdom had trusted more in God and less in military help from the Egyptians, it might have escaped, or at least been treated more leniently; but even this hardly justifies the assertion of the two prophets that the exile was brought about by God as a punishment.

On the other hand, the assertion of the prophets seems to have been accepted as true by many of the exiles, and this enabled them to feel that they had not been abandoned by God and that he was not powerless. It was the continuing belief in God among the exiles that made possible the successful restoration of a Hebrew community round Jerusalem when the return from exile was permitted and encouraged by the Persian empire of Cyrus. Here again, however, modern Christians will not see God as specially moving Cyrus to permit parties of exiles to return. Cyrus had a belief in God not very different from that of the Hebrews, but this is hardly relevant. He took the view that his empire would be stronger if it had the support of the religions of the subject peoples. In this respect his policy differed from that of the earlier empires. What made possible the restoration, then, was not God working through Cyrus, but the inner strength given by God to the exiles who continued to believe in him. It is in this sense that God may be said to have brought about the restoration from exile.

God's chosen people

The Old Testament writers held that the body of people to whom they belonged had been specially chosen by God. In this book they have been spoken of as the Hebrews or Hebrew tribes during the earlier period, and then after the time of Ezra and Nehemiah (about 450 BCE) as the Jews, since by that time their religion had come to have something like its later form. Clearly God had been revealing himself to these people through his inner promptings to Abraham, Moses and countless others. For a time they seem to have thought that God had given them a place in the world superior to that of the other peoples, but the later prophets were coming to see that God had also given them a task, namely, to share what they had learnt about him with the other people of the world. The modern believer might also say that God had given them the task of developing further the imperfect knowledge of himself and his purposes which they had in the earlier days.

Even the later Old Testament writers probably had no knowledge of the important advances in religious thinking that were being made in India and other eastern countries. All they could be aware of were the various forms of polytheism among the surrounding peoples. Thus the immediate task assigned to them was the replacing of this polytheism by belief in God alone. When a religion such as Buddhism is considered, however, the relation to it of biblical religion is more complex, for Buddhism, we believe, has gained some genuine knowledge of God and spiritual matters, but has expressed this in terms of different cosmological and other background thinking. Modern Christians may therefore hold that, while God chose the biblical people for certain purposes, he also chose other peoples for slightly different purposes.

Christians further believe that, when the majority of the Jews of the time failed to accept Jesus as their messiah, it was those Jews who accepted Jesus who retained the status of chosen people, together with the vast numbers of gentiles who joined them. The rejection of Jesus by most of the Jews was primarily a rejection of his conception of messiahship. Many thought of the messiah as a military leader, and this may be said to be the reason for the destruction of Jerusalem by the Romans in 70 CE – a punishment for a false conception. Christians believe that

God forgives sins and still has work for the penitents. This means that God still has a task for today's Jews, though probably not the same as before; but it is not for a Christian to say what this task is. Outside observers, however, see in the contemporary state of Israel a reliance on military power comparable to that which led to the disaster of 70 CE; and at the same time they see a failure to observe the Mosaic law fully, as, for example, when Israelis take over Arab houses without paying for them, since that is stealing.

THE HUMANITY OF JESUS SIX

The General Position

The Chalcedonian creed of 451 CE states clearly that Jesus was truly human. It opens: 'We then, following the Holy Fathers, all with one consent teach people to confess one and the same Son, our Lord Jesus Christ, to be both perfect in divinity and perfect in humanity, truly God and also human with a rational soul and a body, consubstantial with the Father in his divinity and also consubtantial with us in his humanity, wholly like us apart from sin' (quoted with slight changes from W. A. Curtis, A *History of Creeds and Confessions of Faith in Christendom and Beyond*, Edinburgh, 1911, p. 71). I take this credal statement to mean that Jesus had no power to do anything a saintly human being could not do.

Many modern Christians will at once say, 'What about the miracles performed by Jesus?' Behind this question, however, there is a misunderstanding, namely, the view that Jesus performed the miracles by powers which he himself possessed. This is not the biblical understanding of the miracles, however. The Bible asserts the occurrence of many other miracles: the halting of the sun for Joshua and his men, the plagues that affected the

Egyptians, the raising of the dead by Elijah and Elisha, Elisha's feeding of a large number with a few loaves. Likewise in the New Testament works of healing are performed by the early apostles, and Paul is said to have raised a dead man to life (Acts 20.9–12). The biblical view, however, is that all these events are the work of God. Moses prayed to God for the beginning and ending of some of the plagues; but the other events may be regarded as being in some sense a response of God to the prophets, apostles and to Jesus himself. From this it follows that the performing of miracles by Jesus was not through any special powers he possessed, so that he was not a superman or god-man. He was consubstantial with us and wholly like us apart from sin.

The Miracles of Jesus in Detail

There is no great difficulty about the works of healing. It was not only Jesus who performed these, but the twelve apostles and other missioners also healed people. There was a ministry of healing in the early church, which continued off and on; and in recent times this ministry is being recovered in various Christian bodies. Jesus probably had some special gift for healing, which enabled him to deal with more serious cases than his apostles, but it was only a difference of degree, and a few people nowadays seem to have a similar gift. It is also possible that the gospel writers sometimes exaggerated what actually happened.

In three cases Jesus is said to have raised a dead person to life: the daughter of Jairus (Matthew 9.18–26 and parallels); the son of the widow of Nain (Luke 7.11–15); and Lazarus (John 11.1–44). It seems likely that these are no more than acts of healing, and that the persons were in some sort of deep coma which was mistaken for death. In Scotland in 1996 a woman who had been certified dead and placed in a mortuary was found to be still alive. If this can happen with all our advanced medical knowledge, it could certainly have happened in first-century Palestine. Indeed the text gives grounds for thinking that the raising of Eutychus by Paul should be understood in this way, because, although he was taken up as dead, Paul said that there was still life in him (Acts 20.7–12).

In some ways the most outstanding miracle is the changing of water into wine at Cana (John 2). As noted above, John made this the first 'sign' of the achievement of Jesus, because it was a symbol of how Jesus can change something ordinary into something precious in the religion both of individuals and of the contemporary Jewish people as a whole. It is not impossible that what actually happened was that the master of the feast had drunk so much that he was slightly fuddled and mistook the pure water for a fine wine; and the synoptic writers may have suspected this, and for this reason omitted the incident altogether.

The two stories of the feeding of thousands are more mysterious. There may be some exaggeration in the stories, because the writers wanted to show that Jesus could do better than Elisha, who had fed a hundred men with twenty loaves. One possibility is that these feedings were anticipations of the eucharist, so that each person would have only a small piece; and it is noteworthy that John follows his version of the story with a eucharistic discourse (chapter 6). It is also possible that people who had food with them shared it round. Whatever actually happened there is no need to suppose that there was some breach of natural law.

Much the same is true of the other alleged miracles, such as the stilling of a storm and walking on water. In the case of the storm, did the serenity of Jesus restore the confidence of the disciples, or did the tempest suddenly subside, as storms are said to do in the Sea of Galilee? Walking on the water could be a description of swimming, by someone unfamiliar with it, or Jesus could have been in shallow water near the shore. In all these incidents we cannot now know what exactly happened. It is even conceivable that the writers meant the occurrence to be understood symbolically. There is certainly no ground for thinking that something happened contrary to the laws of nature, or that Jesus was able to do things that other saintly persons cannot do.

The Dating of the Mission of Jesus

The four gospels contain little chronological information, but there are one or two indications of dating that can be worked out by scholars and expressed in terms of the years of our Common Era (CE, or AD). The most important of these is the statement of Luke (3.1) that John the Baptist began his mission in the fifteenth year of the emperor Tiberius. There are, however, two ways of translating this into our standard years. It could commence either in August 28 CE or in September/October 27 CE. While the former is not impossible, the latter is preferable as giving longer for John's mission and that of Jesus.

A second small piece of information is given by John (2.20), where the Jews say that the temple in Jerusalem has taken forty-six years to build. The reconstruction under Herod the Great is known to have begun in 19 BCE, so that the earliest date for the Passover at which the statement was made would be 28 CE. This Passover was the first of three mentioned by John in his account of the mission of Jesus, and 28 CE would fit in with what is thought on other grounds to be the most likely date for the crucifixion of Jesus. The Passover is celebrated on the fourteenth day of the Jewish month Nisan, and this day was a Saturday in

THE HUMANITY OF JESUS

the years 30 and 33 CE. The synoptic gospels say that Jesus had his last supper with his disciples on the previous day, Thursday/Friday. Thus the most likely date for the crucifixion is Friday 7 April 30 CE, since 33 CE seems to be too late. In these calculations one has to remember that the Jewish day runs not from midnight to midnight but from sunset to sunset. (This is based on the New Jerusalem Bible, notes on Luke 3.1 and Matthew 26.17, and the chronological table.)

This suggested dating is not certain, of course, but it helps to give us some idea of the course of the missions of John the Baptist and Jesus. It seems most likely that John the Baptist began his mission in summer or autumn 27 CE, and that Jesus went to him either then or in early spring of 28, since he seems to have been himself preaching in Judaea shortly after the Passover of 28.

The fourth gospel mentions five Jewish feasts prior to the Passover before which Jesus was crucified, and at four of these says that Jesus was present. There is every reason for accepting the fourth gospel as here presenting historical data, despite the fact that at many points it has to be understood symbolically, and that it puts discourses into the mouth of Jesus which present not what he actually said but what the writer after long meditation thought was implicit in what he actually said. The historical material presumably came from 'the beloved disciple' who is mentioned at several points in the gospel but not named. He seems to have been an inhabitant of Jerusalem, for he was known to the high priest and was able to introduce Peter into the building in which the discussions were taking place (John 18.16).

At the first of the Passovers where Jesus was present in Jerusalem John says he effected a purification of the temple (John 2.13–22). This is contrary to the synoptics, who say it was at the final Passover; and this is almost certainly the truth, because of the confrontation with the authorities involved in the cleansing. Jesus is then said by John to have gone to a place beside the Jordan and to have engaged in a mission similar to that of John the Baptist (3.22), and later to have returned to Galilee (4.43–5). Next Jesus is said to have gone to Jerusalem for a festival which is not named (5.1), and which might have been that of Pentecost, but is more likely to have been that of Booths or Tabernacles (in October) or of the Dedication (in December). After this the Jews are said to have been hostile to him. Next, while Jesus was engaged in his mission in Galilee, it is said that the Passover was near (6.4), but Jesus does not seem to have gone to this Passover, presumably that of 29 CE. After this on the following feast of Booths Jesus delayed going to Jerusalem, doubtless because of the hostility he was likely to find. Eventually, however, he went 'secretly', but managed to preach in the temple without incurring arrest (7.1–15). He went again to Jerusalem for the feast of the Dedication (December), but soon retreated across the Jordan, though he came back briefly for the raising of Lazarus, before returning to the desert to a place called Ephraim (10.22–40; 11.7, 24). Finally there was the visit to Jerusalem at Passover time which led to his death.

There are difficulties about accepting John's statements as chronologically correct. Thus he says that the changing of the water into wine at Cana (chapter 2) was the first of the 'signs' of what Jesus achieved, but by this he would seem to mean first in importance and not first chronologically. It would also appear that it was for symbolic reasons that he placed the cleansing of the temple during the first Passover attended by Jesus, although it almost certainly happened at the final Passover. One might also ask whether the Passover described by John as 'being near' (6.4) is other than the ones he says Jesus attended. The probability is that it is not one of them, and that for some reason Jesus did not attend; otherwise there would be little time for the mission in Galilee and the visits to Tyre and Caesarea Philippi.

Despite these difficulties John's list of the feasts in Jerusalem attended by Jesus should be accepted. Apart from the final one which led to his death none of these is mentioned by the synoptics. A passage in Luke, however, seems to imply another visit (9.51–6). It speaks of Jesus passing through a Samaritan village and being rejected by the villagers; and Luke treats this as happening on the last journey. Later on this last journey Jesus passes through Jericho (18.35 etc.). Normally, however, one would not go from Samaria to Jerusalem by way of Jericho, since this would involve a descent of several thousand feet and a climb up again of nearly as much. It seems probable, then, that this incident occurred on one of the journeys not specifically mentioned by the synoptics.

All these considerations enable us to give a possible time-table for the mission of Jesus. It is not necessarily correct, but it gives an idea of the course of events and the timing. Jewish months usually overlap two of our months, so that Nisan, for example, is March/April; but for simplicity only the second of our months is named in the following list.

Birth of Jesus in Herod's reign	Before 4 BCE
Beginning of John the Baptist's mission	27 CE, summer or autumn
Jesus is baptized and begins mission	27, autumn, or 28, spring
First Passover of Jesus	28, April
Booths or Dedication	28, October or December
Second Passover (not attended)	29, April
Feast of Booths	29, October

65

Feast of Dedication	29, December
Last Passover	30, April
Crucifixion	30, 7 April

The earliest mission of Jesus was in Judaea near the Jordan, and his move to a mission in Galilee was in late summer or autumn 28.

Family and Early Life

It has been maintained above that the infancy narratives in Matthew and Luke are pictorial presentations of the significance of Jesus. The placing of his birth in Bethlehem supports his claim to be messiah, as do the genealogies of Joseph in Matthew and Luke which make him a descendant of David. (The genealogies are not identical.) Joseph was legally his father by having named him at his circumcision, and he was also socially recognized as his father, since none of the neighbours seem to have known of the virginal conception. He was 'the carpenter's son' (Matthew 13.55). If the virginal conception is taken as a pictorial presentation of the divinity of Jesus, then Joseph was also his physical father, and presumably Jesus was born in Nazareth and spent all his early life there apart from visits to Jerusalem (such as that in Luke's infancy narrative, if there is anything factual in that).

There are a number of references in the gospels to the brothers and sisters of Jesus. In a visit to Nazareth in the course of his mission in Galilee he spoke in the synagogue, and the people were amazed that the local boy should show such wisdom. 'Is this not the carpenter's son? Is not his mother called Mary, and his brothers James and Joses (or Joset or Joseph) and Simon and Jude? And his sisters, are they not all with us?' (Matthew 13.55f.;

cf. Mark 6.2–4). On another occasion he was told that his mother and brothers and sisters were at the back of the crowd and wanting to speak to him; but he took the opportunity to say that his real mother and brothers and sisters were those who did the will of God (Matthew 12.46–50). At this point in his career he may have felt that his family was opposed to his mission. Another passage speaks of his family or relatives (a somewhat vague Greek phrase) going out to restrain him because he was out of his mind (Mark 3.20f.). The likelihood is that this refers primarily to the brothers. In a passage in John (7.2ff.) it is explicitly stated that his brothers did not believe in him, and they urged him to go to a feast in Jerusalem at a time when to go openly would have been dangerous for him. John also records the presence of his mother and brothers at the wedding in Cana and then their return to Capernaum, presumably their permanent home at this time (John 2).

In Christian tradition Mary had no other children after Jesus. While this view might have developed for theological reasons, it is possible that it is factually true. The brothers and sisters would then be children of Joseph by an earlier marriage, and so stepbrothers and stepsisters; but it is also possible, though less likely, that the words are used for cousins. The disbelief of the brothers in the mission of Jesus, too, suggests elder brothers rather than younger brothers, since the latter might have been expected to look up to him. If the visit to Jerusalem at the age of twelve is factual, Joseph was still alive then, but he was presumably dead at the time of the mission of Jesus, since there is no mention of him then.

There is thus no reason for doubting that Jesus had an ordinary childhood in a family, and played with the other boys and girls of Nazareth of about his age. In speaking of the attitude of his contemporaries to John the Baptist and himself he makes use of a comparison with children's games, where some said to others 'we have piped and you have not danced, and we have mourned and you have not wept' (Matthew 11.16f.); and this sounds like a game of weddings and funerals. For his religious upbringing Jesus must have owed much to Mary and Joseph, but he was presumably in some ways a precocious child (as his behaviour during the visit to Jerusalem at the age of twelve suggests). There is nothing, however, to show that he was other than an ordinary village carpenter, following Joseph, until he went to listen to John the Baptist preaching.

There are references in the New Testament to 'James the brother of the Lord', who had a position of leadership in the Christian community in Jerusalem (Acts 12.17; 15.13; 21.18; Galatians 1.19; 2.7, 9). The Epistle of James in the New Testament is sometimes ascribed to him, but the ascription is by no means certain. It is not known, either, whether this James was one of the brothers of Jesus associated with Mary, or a more distant relative.

The Baptism and Call to Mission

Until he was about thirty Jesus lived quietly in Nazareth as a carpenter. The change came when he felt called to go and listen to the preaching of John the Baptist, for he was convinced by what John was saying and accepted baptism. The mission of the Baptist had probably begun in summer or autumn 27. The evangelists are chiefly interested in his witness to the messiahship of Jesus, and give only a slight account of his preaching and virtually nothing about its effect on people. It is therefore surprising to find two references in the book of Acts (18.24f.; 19.1–7) to people who had been baptized by John or his disciples. An

Alexandrian Jew called Apollos appeared in Ephesus preaching about Jesus, although he had not been baptized in the name of Jesus but only with John's baptism; and shortly afterwards Paul found in Ephesus a dozen men who had only known John's baptism.

According to the first gospel John the Baptist put at the centre of his preaching the proclamation that 'the kingdom of heaven is close at hand'. This gospel uses the phrase 'kingdom of heaven' for what the others call the 'kingdom of God', because it follows the pious Jewish practice of not speaking the name of God. The Baptist, however, does not seem to mean the same as Jesus by the phrase. For him the kingdom of God was a time of retribution when people would be punished for their sins. So he urged people 'to flee from the wrath to come', and in particular to repent of their sins and to have them, as it were, washed away by baptism in the Jordan. Baptism was by total immersion. After baptism people were to show in their lives fruits worthy of repentance.

Luke (3.10–14) gives some examples of what John meant by fruits of repentance. People with more clothing or food than they required were to give some away to those in need. Tax-collectors were not to demand more than the proper amount. Soldiers were not to use their position to extract money from people by threats. It is significant that Luke mentions tax-collectors and soldiers, because these were people whom the Jewish authorities regarded as incapable of performing their religious duties on account of their relation to non-Jews. The tax-collectors worked for syndicates of Roman businessmen to whom the government had committed the collection of taxes; and the soldiers presumably had some minor positions in the Roman army. According to strict Jews that prevented them from performing their religious duties as Jews. This indicates that many of those who flocked to hear the Baptist preaching were ordinary people who felt excluded from their religion.

When Jesus went to listen to John he was so impressed by the preaching that, like many other people there, he went forward to baptism. As he came out of the water it is said that he saw the Holy Spirit in the form of a dove descending upon him. It is further stated that he at once went into solitude for forty days and was tempted of the devil. This is pictorial language and need not be taken literally, but it presents important facts about Jesus. First of all it means that he felt some sort of call to mission; but the probability is that he had not yet come to the understanding which he finally reached of his own personal mission. Presumably he was meditating on such matters in his period of solitude. The synoptics place this period immediately after the baptism, but, if the fourth gospel is correct in saying that his first mission was in Judaea, the time for thinking things out could have come between that and the later mission in Galilee. Jesus may well have become a disciple of John for a time, though this is not mentioned. The early mission in Judaea, however, looks like a continuation of John's mission, since people were baptized by disciples of John who had followed Jesus.

In the first and fourth gospels the Baptist is said to have recognized the messiahship of Jesus, but this is very unlikely. John may have met Jesus previously, however, since they were relatives through their mothers, and may have seen in him a young man of great promise. He could hardly have gone further, however, since Jesus himself almost certainly did not yet know the precise form his mission and his activity were finally to take.

Some problems are raised by the fact that the baptism was a baptism for the remission of sins, whereas at many points in the New Testament Jesus is said to be sinless (2 Corinthians 5.21; Hebrews 4.15; 7.26; 1 Peter 2.22; 1 John 3.5). To say that someone else is sinless, however, is different from claiming sinlessness for oneself. The latter would be a form of spiritual arrogance, like that of the Pharisee whom Jesus compares with the tax-collector, for he prided himself on his fulfilment of the law (Luke 18.9–14). When Jesus was addressed by a rich young man as 'Good master', his reply was, 'Why do you call me good? None is good except God' (Mark 10.17f.; Luke 18.18f.). When he was baptized, therefore, Jesus may have felt that he was repenting of minor shortcomings which others had not noticed, or he may have felt that he was involved somehow in the sinfulness of his people.

Latterly Jesus seems to have come to regard the Baptist as the forerunner sent to prepare the way for him. After answering a question to the Baptist's disciples he talked to the crowds about the Baptist himself, and quoted a verse which spoke of God sending a messenger to prepare the way (Malachi 3.1). It is unlikely that Jesus himself used the verse in Isaiah (40.3) as quoted in the gospels: 'the voice of one crying in the wilderness, Prepare ye the way of the Lord.' This is based on the Greek of the Septuagint; but Jesus would only be familiar with the Hebrew Bible, where the wilderness is not the place of crying but the place for the preparation of the way; that is, the Hebrew reads: 'The voice of one crying, Prepare in the wilderness . . .'.

It seems certain that at the time of his baptism Jesus received a call to mission of some sort. Various passages in the gospels make it likely that he first thought that his call was to be a prophet, with a message to be proclaimed to his contemporaries. Thus later, in the course of his mission in Galilee, he compared himself to the prophet Jonah announcing the destruction of Nineveh – a message that was accepted by the Ninevites (Matthew 12.41; Luke 11.32). Again, when Jesus was asked, on behalf of the Baptist, whether he was the one to come, he replied by pointing to what was happening in the course of his mission, namely, the blind seeing, the lame walking and so on (Matthew 11.5; Luke 7.22). This appears to be a reference to passages in Isaiah (29.18f.; 35.5f.; 61.1), but these refer to the great day of the Lord when he will save his people, and have no explicit reference to a messiah. Similarly in a sermon at Nazareth (Luke 4.16–30) he bases himself on a passage in Isaiah (61.1f.) which speaks of the day of the Lord and the year of God's favour. The absence of the mention of the messiah fits in well with what seems to have been central in the early part of his mission in Galilee, namely, the proclamation that the reign of God is at hand. It was also necessary to be careful in the use of the term messiah, since there was a widespread desire for a messiah who would be a military leader.

Jesus eventually came to believe that he had a mission to reform the Jewish religion and perhaps also to effect the redemption of all humanity, but he did not cease to think of himself as a prophet. On the occasion of a visit to Nazareth he complained that a prophet is not without honour except in his own country (John 4.44; Matthew 13.57 and parallels). Even as he was preparing for the final visit to Jerusalem and the confrontation with the Jewish authorities he remarked that it was not fitting that a prophet should die outside Jerusalem (Luke 13.33). Other people also thought of him as a prophet. When the people of Nain saw the widow's son restored to life, they said that a great prophet had risen up among them. Likewise, the man who invited him to a dinner party at which a woman of the town anointed his feet thought that, if this man had been a prophet, he would have known what sort of woman this was (Luke 7.39).

The Temptations of Jesus

Soon after his baptism, but perhaps not until after the short period of mission beside the Jordan, Jesus spent some time in solitude away from human habitation. Here he is said to have been visited and tempted by the devil, though the so-called 'temptations' do not seem to mean that something evil appeared attractive to him. They were rather a thinking out of some aspects of his mission, and of course they are described in pictorial terms. They are essentially what we would now call inner experiences, but the people of New Testament times had to give such experiences an external form. All the replies to the devil are quotations from the book of Deuteronomy, and this suggests that Jesus had been meditating on passages from the Old Testament.

The first temptation (Matthew 4.1–4; Luke 4.1–4) followed on a period of fasting, supposedly of forty days. Because he was hungry the tempter suggested to him that he should use his messianic power to change stones into bread. To this Jesus replied by quoting some words of Moses, 'Man shall not live by bread alone, but by every word that proceeds from the mouth of God' (Deuteronomy 8. 3). Moses was speaking to the Hebrew people after they had reached the border of the promised land, but before they had crossed the Jordan. He emphasized the need to keep all God's commands, and reminded them how God had provided manna for food in the wilderness, and had kept their clothes from wearing out.

How would Jesus see this as applying to himself? He was proposing to set out on a mission. That would involve giving up his work as a carpenter by which he was earning his living, and he would have no savings account to fall back on. Should he try to earn a little extra before setting out on the mission? He decided that the primary thing was to do God's will, and that somehow his material needs would be provided for. This was the attitude he recommended to other people in the Sermon on the Mount (Matthew 6.25–33). 'Do not worry about what you will eat or drink, or about what you will wear; look at the birds, how God feeds them; look at the lilies, how God clothes them beautifully; and you are of more value than birds and lilies.' This trustful attitude was perhaps in part linked with conditions in Galilee at that time, for these were very different from those in our contemporary world. There would be no hotels or guest houses in the villages, but there was a tradition that, if a stranger had to spend a night in a village, someone would offer him basic hospitality. This seems usually to have happened when Jesus himself went preaching, and also when his disciples went in twos and threes. Things may have been different when he was accompanied by a dozen disciples and a number of women followers, but the latter had money which they used for food and other necessities. The result of the first temptation, then, was that Jesus decided to set out at once on his mission, trusting to have his basic needs supplied somehow.

Another temptation, second in Matthew (4.5–7) and third in Luke (4.9–12), is also rejected on the basis of a quotation from the same discourse of Moses. The tempter takes Jesus in imagination to a pinnacle of the temple and says that, if he flings himself down, no harm will happen to him, for it has been written: 'God will give his angels charge over you to protect you, and they will carry you in their hands to prevent you dashing your foot against a stone' (Psalm 91.11f.). This has sometimes been taken literally as a miracle to impress the crowds and cause them to believe; but that is ridiculous. The relevance of the tempter's suggestion is much deeper, as a reference to the quotation will make clear.

In his reply Jesus quoted the words of Moses: 'You shall not tempt the Lord your God' (Deuteronomy 6.16). These are linked to an incident which occurred shortly after the Hebrews left Egypt (Exodus 17.1–7). They had reached a place called Rephidim, where there was no water, and thought they were all going to die of thirst. They blamed Moses, but God showed Moses a way of getting water, and the crisis ended. Moses then called the place Massah (temptation) and Meribah (strife), because the Hebrews strove with God and tempted God, saying, 'Is the Lord among us or not?' Thus, in this sense of the word, to 'tempt' God is to ask whether he is supporting one or not; and that is virtually to doubt his existence or power.

The idea expressed in the above passage from Exodus is one that occurs frequently in the Old Testament, namely, that God protects upright people, especially those going about his work. It was almost certainly becoming apparent to Jesus, as his conception of his mission developed in his mind, that in the course of it he would raise the opposition and hostility of the Jewish authorities, and as a result would be likely to suffer at their hands. Would God protect him from all harm in such a situation? The answer to the tempter thus meant that, whatever sufferings he had to bear, he would continue to trust in God. This means that the rejection of this temptation was in fact a first acceptance of his passion. On the cross he said, 'My God, why hast thou forsaken me?' and these are the first words of Psalm 22, which ends on a positive note; and other words of Jesus on the cross show that he continued to believe in the Father. If the temptation occurred after the arrest of John the Baptist, this would be another relevant point.

By way of parenthesis it might be noted that this obsolete meaning of 'tempt' and 'temptation' is found in one or two other passages of the Authorized Version. The most obvious one is in the Lord's Prayer (Matthew 6.13). Here it seems probable that the clause 'lead us not into temptation' does not mean 'keep us from being tempted' but 'keep us from tempting or doubting God'; and some people might feel that this is a more appropriate prayer. Another instance of this former meaning is in Psalm 98.8, 9, where there is a reference to 'the day of temptation in the wilderness, when your fathers tempted me and saw my works'; and as a result of their doubts these people were excluded from the promised land.

The remaining temptation (Matthew 4.8–10; Luke 4.5–8) was about the achieving of power. The tempter took him in imagination to a high mountain, showed him all the kingdoms of the earth, and said he would give all these to Jesus if he worshipped him, the tempter. Jesus replied with another quotation from the discourse of Moses to the effect that God alone was to be worshipped and served (Deuteronomy 6.13). Moses was warning the Hebrews that, after they were settled in Palestine, they were not to worship the local deities. It is not obvious, however, how all this applies to Jesus. For one thing it is not clear what worshipping the tempter or devil would amount to in practice.

One possibility is that, if Jesus had put himself at the head of those who were preparing for a military rebellion against the Romans, he might have achieved some astounding successes through his gifts for leading and inspiring people. It is unlikely, however, that Jesus thought of the matter in quite this way, since he was looking towards something deeper than merely getting rid of Roman rule; and he may have been more aware than many of the strength of Rome. A more likely possibility is that Jesus thought that, if he somewhat softened his message so as not to offend the Jewish authorities but to gain their support, this would greatly strengthen his nation to achieve important things in the world, either militarily or in other ways.

By rejecting the tempter's suggestion Jesus was in fact deciding to do God's will as he understood it without regarding the immediate consequences. Worshipping the tempter or devil would seem to amount to looking at a desired result and calculating how it might be achieved; and that would be a kind of worship of power.

The Proclamation of the Reign of God

The main part of the mission of Jesus was that in Galilee, probably from about summer 28 until April, 30 CE. During this period he went round the villages of Galilee preaching in the synagogues. Sometimes he sent disciples in pairs to prepare the way for him, as it were. His base was probably in Capernaum in the house of Simon Peter, though his own family also seem to have had a house there. He presented himself as a prophet with a message to proclaim.

The heart of the message was that the reign of God was at hand. The Authorized Version speaks of 'the kingdom of God' (and in Matthew of 'the kingdom of heaven' as noted above); but the reign or rule of God seems more appropriate, since there was no suggestion of a territorial kingdom. It was a deeper relation of human beings to God. John the Baptist had also spoken of the coming reign of God, but for him it had been primarily a pouring out of God's anger in the punishment of sins. This was also present in the teaching of Jesus, but he placed more emphasis on the positive aspect. In one account it is said that he called on people to repent of their sins and believe the good news (Matthew 4.17; Mark 1.15). A fuller statement is given in Luke's account of his visit to the synagogue in Nazareth (4.16–30). Here he quoted from Isaiah (61.1f.; 58.6): 'The spirit of the Lord is upon me, and he has anointed me to bring good news to the poor; he has sent me to announce release to the prisoners and sight to the blind, to set the oppressed free, to proclaim the acceptable year of the Lord.' These activities are to be understood symbolically, although before this point in the mission sight may have been restored to a blind person. More important than the actual restoring of sight was the bringing of a new vision to those who were spiritually blind; and the releasing of prisoners and freeing of the oppressed was the releasing of those imprisoned by false beliefs or suffering from them in some way.

While this positive side was dominant in the teaching of Jesus, he also spoke of an impending disaster which was to be seen as God's punishment of the sins of past and present generations. All the righteous blood shed in the past, from that of Abel to that of the priest Zacharias, was to be paid for by this generation (Matthew 23.34–6). In speaking of such matters Jesus sometimes seems to have used the phrase 'the end of the world'; and some people have thought that this meant the end of the historical process as such. Almost certainly, however, Jesus did not mean this, for he also spoke of himself as the initiator of a new covenant, that is, of a new relationship between God and human beings. He may also have foreseen something like what happened to Jerusalem and Judaism in 70 CE, for that was in a sense the end of the world the Jews had been living in for centuries.

Scholars now tell us that most of the first-century Palestinian Jews felt that they were still in exile because they were under foreign rule. Various leading groups had a deep concern to preserve Jewish identity and Jewish tradition; but they tended to do this in ways that reduced the numbers of those they accepted as Jews. Many also looked forward to and prepared for a military rising against the Romans; and this tendency led to the catastrophic war of 66–70 CE, and so to the end of the semiautonomous Jewish state, the partial destruction of Jerusalem and the transformation of what was left into a Roman city, Aelia Capitolina.

Jesus was opposed to the leaders – Pharisees, Sadducees and others – who were trying to preserve Jewish identity. They had a conception of a 'practising Jew' which tended to overemphasize such matters as ritual cleanliness, and so to exclude those who, because of the nature of their daily work, could not fulfil the requirements. Among the contemporaries of Jesus many felt excluded from their religion, and this was one of the reasons why they flocked to listen to John the Baptist and then to Jesus. It was of such people that Jesus was thinking when he said he was sent to the lost sheep of the house of Israel. He wanted them to feel that, as soon as they repented of their moral faults, they were loved and accepted by the God of Israel. Although he said that he himself was sent only to those lost sheep, he clearly envisaged the presence of non-Jews in the new community of Israel which he hoped to bring about. He said that many would come from east and west and sit down with Abraham, Isaac and Jacob in the kingdom of God (Matthew 8.11f.; 23.34–6).

Jesus was deeply versed in the thinking of the Old Testament, especially the later parts, and he also shared much of the outlook of his contemporary Jews. He felt, however, that in important respects their leaders were leading them astray. He therefore saw his mission to be the bringing about of a transformation of the religion of Israel. This was why he spoke of being sent to the lost sheep of the house of Israel. He was not thinking of creating a new world religion, though that in a sense was what he achieved. He wanted to develop the religion of Israel to what God had intended it to be; and by so doing he would finally achieve (in a spiritual sense) the return from exile for which many of his contemporaries were hoping. He probably also saw it as a kind of second exodus from an alien land. For modern Christians, however, the most intelligible description is the inauguration of a new covenant between God and the human race along the lines which had been foreseen by Jeremiah (31.31–4).

By the time of his death Jesus was fully aware that he was in a sense acting for God. In his institution of the eucharist he saw his death as the sacrifice which would inaugurate the new covenant. When he spoke of himself as 'the good shepherd', he was claiming a role which in the Old Testament had been God's (e.g. Psalm 23). There was no question of starting something completely new. Before things could move forward an appreciable number of existing Jews must accept the teaching of Jesus, follow him and so constitute a new reformed Israel. It would be for this reformed Israel to accept gentiles as fellow members of the community of worshippers of God.

The Culmination of the Mission

Jesus went to Jerusalem a few days before the Passover of 30 CE. He felt strongly that what he was about to do should be done in the full glare of publicity. Much of the value of his actions would be lost if he met a hole-in-the-corner death, such as had befallen John the Baptist. It was not right, he thought, that a prophet should die except in Jerusalem (Luke 13.33).

Near the beginning of his time in Jerusalem he brought about what is called the cleansing of the temple; in other words he drove out those who were selling animals for sacrifice and over-turned the tables of the money-changers who were providing the appropriate coins for the payment of temple dues (Matthew 21.12f.; Mark 11.15–17; Luke 19.45f.). This was not because he thought there should be no commercial dealings in the temple, but because he thought that the Jewish authorities were placing far too much emphasis on the sacrificial system and neglecting more important aspects of their religion. These latter had been stated by the prophet Micah, for example, as 'doing justly, loving mercy, and walking humbly with God' (Micah 6.8). The cleansing of the temple was something the authorities could not ignore. It was a deliberate confrontation with them.

The details of the final week need not be further considered here, but one small point may be mentioned. Jesus, seeing a fig tree, looked for fruit and found none (although fig trees sometimes retain some of the previous year's fruits until the spring); then later the disciples found the tree dead. This may be factually true, but more important is its symbolic truth. Jesus came looking for a response from the Jews of his day, but received virtually none from the leaders, so that their religion could be regarded as dead.

What seems to be uppermost in his mind was that God wanted him to act out the sacrifice needed for the inauguration of the new covenant. It was obviously a bitter cup to drink, and he shrank from it; but in the end he realized that he had to go on with it. In his last supper with his disciples he set before them the form of what has become the Christian eucharist. In this the bread and wine become symbols of his body and blood which he was to yield up at his crucifixion.

The Resurrection

A brief summary of all the New Testament statements about the resurrection of Jesus is given in an appendix. It will be seen that there are some discrepancies in them, the chief one being whether the first appearances were made at Jerusalem or in

Galilee. These discrepancies are not a reason for rejecting the accounts but rather one for accepting them. Historians normally find that when a large number of people share experiences, their descriptions of them tend to differ.

It is clear that, not merely was the tomb found empty, but there was no dead body anywhere. Had the followers of Jesus known of his dead body somewhere they could not have proclaimed the resurrection, and had the opponents known of it they would certainly have produced it. The early Christians believed that the body of Jesus had been taken up into heaven, but this implies that heaven is a place up in the sky, and that is impossible for modern believers, since for them heaven is somehow beyond space and time. To go upwards physically would only take one to the moon or Mars. What then happened to the body of Jesus? It has been suggested that robbers, thinking that there might be jewels on the body of a king, took it from the tomb and then left it to the fowls of the air, so that nothing remained except unidentifiable bones. It seems unlikely that this could have happened without someone else being aware of it and reporting it. It is best to admit that what happened to the physical body of Jesus is a mystery which we cannot now solve.

Scholars have spoken of the body which appeared to the early Christians as the 'resurrection body'. It looked like a physical body, but it could do things a physical body could not do. It could enter a room through closed doors, and it could vanish into the air as it did at Emmaus. Strangely, too, it was not always immediately recognized as being Jesus. Mary Magdalene at the tomb thought at first that it was the gardener (John 20.14–16); and the Emmaus pair only recognized Jesus when he broke bread at a meal (Luke 24.16–21). There is no difficulty, of course, in saying that the resurrection body was taken up into heaven, and that Jesus is now seated at the right hand of God. Such statements are to be understood pictorially or symbolically. We can also say that on Easter day Jesus had already entered into eternal life. What can be affirmed about the resurrection with absolute certainty is that it brought about a complete change in the lives of the apostles and of the other followers of Jesus.

TRUE ONENESS OF THE TRIUNE GOD

In today's world, where ordinary Christians are more and more meeting believers in other religions, such as Muslims, it is necessary for them to be able to explain that the God they believe in is one God, even while they also believe that Jesus is divine. For this to be possible it is necessary that trinitarian doctrine should be stated in much simpler terms than those commonly used by theologians. The present chapter is an attempt to present the doctrine in a form that can be comprehended and used by ordinary Christians.

The Divinity of Jesus

First of all it is important to understand why the obviously human Jesus is also to be regarded as divine. Belief in the virgin birth may have helped simple-minded believers to think of him as 'son of God' because he had no human father; but the virgin birth does not make him divine. Hundreds of millions of Muslims believe in the virgin birth because it is asserted in the Qur'an; but at the same time they deny the divinity. In pre-Christian times, too, as we know from the Bible and other sources, the term 'son of God' could be applied to various human beings, and the Bible even speaks of the sons and daughters of God (Isaiah 43.6), while the Christian church holds that those who are baptized become sons and daughters of God. We therefore have to look elsewhere for the reason for regarding Jesus as divine.

The basic reason for holding Jesus to be divine is the character of what he achieved in the world. It is difficult to give a concise account of this achievement in modern terms, and it is therefore better to look at the various terms used in the New Testament to describe it. Jesus is the redeemer of the world, the saviour of the world, the good shepherd who gives his life for the sheep, the one who reconciles human beings with God, and the inaugurator of a new covenant. These are the chief ways in which the achievement of Jesus is described in the New Testament, and they may now be looked at in more detail.

In considering what exactly is meant by the redemption of the world through Jesus it is helpful to look at some quotations from the New Testament. Paul writing to Titus (2.14) spoke of 'our saviour Jesus Christ, who gave himself for us that he might redeem us from all iniquity, and purify unto himself a peculiar people, zealous of good works'. In another passage he speaks of God the Father 'having predestinated us unto the adoption of children by Jesus Christ to himself . . . to the praise and glory of his grace, wherein he has made us accepted in the beloved, in whom we have redemption through his blood and forgiveness of sins' (Ephesians 1.5–7; cf. Colossians 1.14). Other statements by Paul are: 'Christ has redeemed us from the curse of the law, being made a curse for us' (Galatians 3.13); and 'when the fullness of the time was come, God sent forth his son, made of a woman, made under the law, to redeem those that were under the law, that we might receive the adoption of sons' (Galatians 4.4f.).

THE ONENESS OF GOD

Finally there is a statement ascribed to Jesus himself: 'the Son of Man came not to be ministered unto but to minister, and to give his life as a ransom for many' (Matthew 20.28). The Greek word for 'ransom' in the last quotation is *lutron*, which is basically the money paid to buy a slave's freedom; the corresponding verb is used in the letter to Titus, and a verbal noun (*apolutrosis*) in the letter to the Ephesians. The two quotations from the letter to the Galatians have the verb *exagorazein*, whose basic meaning is 'buying from', but it is often used for the paying of money to ransom slaves. There is no Greek noun for 'redeemer' in the New Testament.

The mission of Jesus was not simply to teach people that, when they repent of their sins, God forgives them, for this forgiveness was already familiar to the later Old Testament writers. The slavery from which metaphorically they were to be ransomed was what was involved in 'being under the law' or suffering 'the curse of the law'; and in place of this they were to have the adoption of children of God, and to become a people purified and zealous of good works. What does all this amount to? The Hebrew people had been placed under the law when God revealed it to Moses; and this implied that they were to be judged in respect of their fulfilment or breaking of the law. This law thus came to them, as it were, from without; it was imposed upon them. It was not something they had chosen for themselves. The followers of Jesus, however, through his death and resurrection came to have a new status as sons and daughters of God. They were still expected to live according to God's law, and were given strength to enable them to do this, but the law came to them, as it were, from within themselves because of their filial relationship. The payment made to ransom them was the mission of Jesus in the world and above all his death. Belief in his resurrection, together with the working in them of the Holy Spirit, made it easier for them to live without breaking the law.

Not much is gained on this point by looking at the Old Testament. In the Authorized Version the word 'redeemer' is used to translate the Hebrew *go'el*. According to Hebrew law and custom the *go'el* was the nearest male relative, who was to be the avenger of blood, if necessary, and more generally a defender and protector of the person in question. The translation 'redeemer' is said to go back to Saint Jerome, who had used it because it had been used of the messiah by Jewish rabbis (New Jerusalem Bible, note on Job 19.25). In a speech to the people he was leading Moses said that the Lord 'has brought you out with a mighty hand and has redeemed you out of the house of bondage, even . . . Egypt' (Deuteronomy 7.8). The basic meaning of the verb used here is 'to free', but this does not help in understanding the achievement of Jesus.

There are numerous references in the New Testament to Jesus as 'saviour' (*soter*) and to his work of 'saving' or 'salvation'; but these do not help much in understanding what precisely he achieved. Thus in Luke's gospel (19.10) it is said that 'the Son of Man is come to seek and to save that which was lost'. In Paul's first letter to Timothy (1.15) he says that 'Christ Jesus came into the world to save sinners.' The various New Testament writers seem to assume that their readers know what is meant by 'being saved'. At one place Paul goes a little further and says: 'God commends his love towards us in that while we were yet sinners Christ died for us; much more then, being now justified by his beloved, we shall be saved from wrath through him' (Romans 5.8, 9). From the Holy Spirit Christians received power to overcome sin, but this did not mean that they became perfect and wholly without sin. Perhaps we could link this up with the discussion of redemption and say that 'being saved' meant passing from the condition of being under the law to that of being adopted children of God.

The belief that human beings have, as it were, a divine shepherd comes from the Old Testament. The best known passage is Psalm 23, which begins: 'The Lord is my shepherd; I shall not want; he makes me to lie down in green pastures.' Another is in Psalm 95 (verse 7): 'for he is our God, and we are the people of his pasture and the sheep of his hand'. Jesus may have had this conception in mind when he claimed to be the good shepherd who knows his sheep and lays down his life for them (John 10.14f.). On one occasion (Matthew 15.24) Jesus said that he was sent only to the lost sheep of the house of Israel; but, as has already been seen, this does not mean that the religious changes he was hoping to bring about were to be restricted to the Jews. It was a statement about his own personal mission, and implied that the first priority was to bring into existence a body of Jewish people who had experienced his redemption and salvation, and who would be the core and foundation for a future church. He made this plain when he said: 'other sheep I have which are not of this fold; them also must I bring and they shall hear my voice, and there shall be one fold and one shepherd' (John 10.16). His assertion that 'many shall come from the east and the west, and shall sit down with Abraham, Isaac and Jacob in the kingdom of heaven' (Matthew 8.11) followed on his healing of the servant of a Roman centurion; and this man's faith was so great that Jesus said, 'I have not found so great faith, no, not in Israel' (8.19; cf. Luke 7.2–10).

A rather different description of the achievement of Jesus was given by Paul in his second letter to the Corinthians (5.18f.): 'all things are of God, who has reconciled us to himself by Jesus Christ, and has given to us the ministry of reconciliation, to wit, that God was in Christ reconciling the world unto himself, not imputing their trespasses unto them; and has committed unto us the word of reconciliation'. Somewhat similar ideas are expressed in the letter to the Colossians (1.19–22). The basic thought here seems to be that in the relations between God and human beings there was a kind of barrier, and that this was removed by the death of Jesus on the cross. Perhaps people felt that, although God had forgiven them, he still remembered that they had once sinned.

Lastly, there is the conception of Jesus as the mediator of a new covenant. This is something which was foreseen by the prophet Jeremiah (31.31–4): 'Behold the days come, says the Lord, that I will make a new covenant with the house of Israel and the house of Judah; not according to the covenant that I made with their fathers on the day that I took them by the hand to bring them out of the land of Egypt, which my covenant they broke, although I was a husband to them. But this shall be the covenant that I shall make with the house of Israel. After those days, says the Lord, I will put my law in their inward parts and write it in their hearts; and will be their God and they shall be my people. And they shall teach no more every man his neighbour, and every man his brother, saying, Know the Lord; for they shall all know me from the least of them unto the greatest of them, says the Lord; for I will forgive their iniquity and will remember their sin no more.'

Jesus must have been aware of this passage in Jeremiah, and in his institution of the eucharist is said to have spoken of the wine as 'the blood of the new covenant' (Matthew 26.28; Mark 14.24; Luke 22.20; 1 Corinthians 11.25; 'new' is omitted in some texts). At one point Paul speaks of himself and his colleagues as 'ministers of the new covenant' (2 Corinthians 2.6). Jesus, however, is not reported to have used the word 'covenant' on other occasions, although he saw the basic task of his mission as the establishment of a new relationship between human beings and God. He could thus regard the eucharistic wine as a symbol of the blood shed as a sacrifice for the formal inauguration of the new covenant.

This idea of a new covenant was taken up and worked out further by the writer of the epistle to the Hebrews (8.6): 'But now has (Jesus) obtained a more excellent ministry [i.e. than that of previous high priests] by how much also he is the mediator of a better covenant, which was established upon better promises.' He then goes on to quote Jeremiah. There are further references to the new covenant later in the epistle (10.16f.; 12.24; 13.20). In particular Jesus is spoken of as the high priest who has ratified the covenant by the shedding of his own blood (9.11–28). When the original covenant had to be completed under Moses, the blood of calves and goats had to be sacrificed, and so for the new covenant there had also to be a sacrifice of blood. At the same time there was in the new covenant what was spoken of as the adoption of sons.

Most English-speaking Christians are probably unaware of all that is said about the new covenant, since the Authorized Version mostly uses the translation 'testament'.

In the epistle to the Hebrews 'covenant' is retained, and even there it becomes 'testament' in one passage (9.15–20). The Latin translation of the Greek *diatheke* was *testamentum*, and this may have been adequate; but the English 'testament' completely conceals the meaning. What we call the Old and New Testaments of the Bible should really be the Old and New Covenants.

These are the various ways in which the early Christians thought of the achievement of Jesus, and they lead to the question, How did they come to think of him as divine? The resurrection experiences of the first followers clearly had much to do with this, but these experiences did not in themselves make him divine. They showed that he was still alive and already in some sort of eternal life, and not merely restored to temporal life; but that was not divinity. In the course of the resurrection experiences, however, they came to understand better his conception of his messiahship. Jesus was far from being the messiah many of his contemporaries were hoping for, namely, a victorious leader against the Romans. He was also more than a messiah calling the Jews to a fuller and better fulfilment of the demands of the Mosaic law. He was a messiah calling them and all other human beings to a new and deeper relationship with God, described as the adoption of sons and the inauguration of a new covenant.

The Christians of New Testament times did not come anywhere near the theological subtlety of the later doctrine of the second hypostasis of the Trinity. One Old Testament passage they applied to Jesus was Psalm 110.1, which says: 'The Lord said unto my Lord, Sit thou at my right hand until I make thine enemies thy footstool'; and this would mean that Jesus was in some sense God's right-hand man, achieving something for God. It was also believed that on the fortieth day after the resurrection Jesus had appeared to his followers and had ascended into heaven; and this would imply that he was in some sense with God. In Colossians 1.15–20 Paul speaks of Jesus as 'the image of the unseen God', and then describes his activities in the cosmic process. The clearest statement in the New Testament, however, of the divinity of Jesus is in the first chapter of the fourth gospel. There John speaks of him as the Word or Logos of God. The Greek word *logos* suggests something primarily intellectual, but the moral and spiritual side of human nature must also have been included. This ties up with the Old Testament teaching that God made human beings in his own image. Thus John was implying that what was humanlike in God was given full and complete expression in the life of Jesus. After speaking of the role of the Logos in creation, he goes on to say that those who receive Jesus as Logos thereby become the children of God; that is, they enter into the new and deeper relationship with God the Father.

For modern Christians, then, the divinity of Jesus is based on his achieving his task as messiah of opening up a new and deeper relationship of human beings to God, and especially on the fact that in the closing events of his life he gave the fullest possible manifestation of the outgoing love of God for humanity. In Jesus we see love accepting the most extreme suffering in order to promote the welfare of others. We can then regard such love as an expression of the love of God for human beings, even though we also hold that God in himself cannot experience suffering. God in himself may also be spoken of as God in heaven; but, because human beings have been created in God's image, there is something of the divine in them in this earthly life. This enables us to say that in Jesus we have in its fullness the earthly form of the divine love.

In the light of such an understanding of the divinity of Jesus it is also worth considering whether there is not something of the divine in those we regard as saints. Could it be that the difference between them and Jesus is not one of kind but of degree? This would make a lot of sense, and it would be in line with the teaching that God created human beings in his own image, for that implies that there is something of the divine in them. It would also link up with the belief that baptized Christians become the sons and daughters of God.

The Threefoldness of the One God

It now seems unfortunate that in the sixteenth century the English word 'person' should have been used to translate the Latin *persona*. In the sixteenth century 'person' may have been adequate, though it is difficult to be certain about that. In the course of time words change their meanings, and the predominant meaning of 'person' is now an individual human being; and the three hypostases of God (to use the Greek word) are not even something like three individual human beings. 'Person', of course, is by no means the only word that has changed its meaning. The Holy Ghost is far from being anything like what we now mean by a ghost. A collect in the Prayer Book of the Church of England begins: 'Prevent us, O Lord, in all our doings with thy most gracious favour'; but it means almost the opposite of what we now mean by 'prevent'. When Paul says that 'our conversation is in heaven' (Philippians 3.30) he means rather something like citizenship (*politeuma*). Because of the current meaning of the word 'person' it should be rigorously avoided in trinitarian discussions, since it makes it almost impossible to show the unity of God. The anglicized Greek word 'hypostasis' may be retained, since its meaning is somewhat vague; but even this word will not be of much use to ordinary Christians trying to explain their belief in the oneness of God to non-Christian neighbours.

Traditionally it has been held that the Father created, the Son redeemed and the Spirit sanctified; and so creating, redeeming and sanctifying may be accepted as the main forms of activity of each hypostasis, although there are also others. The creating by the Father includes not merely his initiation of the cosmic process, but also his continuing control of it in some respects, including his creation of each human being.

The redeeming by the Son includes all that was achieved by Jesus through his mission, death and resurrection. To the Spirit is to be attributed not merely the sanctifying of believers, but also all the activities of God within human beings, as these were described in Chapter 4. It should also be remembered that, although the Holy Spirit came to the early Christians in a special way on the day of Pentecost, his activity stretched back into the past; as the creed says, 'he spoke through the prophets'.

A better way for ordinary people of speaking of the various forms of divine activity would be to speak of God as performing three roles. The word 'role' is not all that different from the Latin *persona*, because this was first of all an actor's mask (through which sound came), and then a role in a play. The three roles, of course, would primarily describe God's activity. If one wanted to speak of his being or nature, the word 'aspect' might be a possibility, and comes closer to 'hypostasis'.

It should also be noted that the three roles were not so clearly distinguished in the New Testament as they were in the credal formulations of the later Greek theologians. Thus in the fourth gospel (John 1) the Logos is said to have had a central place in the creation of the world, which is the work of the Father. Where one would expect Paul to speak of the indwelling divine power in him as the Spirit, he says, 'I live, yet not I, Christ lives in me' (Galatians 2.29); and John (1 John 2.1) says that in Jesus we have a paraclete with the Father, although it is the Spirit that is usually spoken of as the Paraclete.

In defending the oneness of God, then, the ordinary Christian could say that God has different roles to perform, and that in the past these have been described as different parts or aspects of his being. God is a single being, however, and these parts and aspects run into one another, and are not so distinct as traditional formulations suggest.

APPENDIX:
The Post-resurrection Appearances

Matthew 28.1–6	Two women at the tomb; there is an earthquake; an angel rolls away the stone and says Jesus is risen. (This implies that the body was moved before the stone was rolled away.)
28.7, 8, 16–20	The women are told to tell the disciples that Jesus is risen and that they are to go to Galilee; they go to Galilee and see Jesus at a mountain; then are told to make disciples of all nations.
28.9, 10	Jesus meets the (two?) women; they hold his feet; he tells them to tell 'his brothers' to go to Galilee.
Mark 16.1–6	Three women at the tomb; the stone already rolled away; a young man tells them Jesus has risen.
16.7, 8	The women are told to tell the disciples to go to Galilee, where they will see Jesus.
16.9–18	Jesus appears (a) to Mary Magdalene, (b) to two disciples (at Emmaus ?) and (c) to the eleven, who are told to proclaim the gospel.

16.19, 20   Jesus 'after he had spoken unto them was taken up into heaven and sat at the right hand of God'; the disciples go out preaching.

Luke
24.1–12   Several women go to the tomb; the stone is already rolled away; two men tell the women that Jesus has risen; the women tell the disciples, who disbelieve; Peter goes to the tomb.

24.13–35   Two disciples go to Emmaus; Jesus joins them, explains the scriptures to them, then vanishes; on return to Jerusalem the two are told that Jesus has appeared to Peter (but this is not described).

24.36–48   Jesus appears to the disciples, the eleven and others, in Jerusalem; he shows his hands and his feet (but wounds are not mentioned); he asks for food and eats some fish; he says the suffering of the messiah was foretold in scripture.

24.49   Jesus is going to send the Holy Spirit; the disciples are to remain in Jerusalem.

24.50f.   Jesus leads them to Bethany; in blessing them he is carried up into heaven.

John
20.1–10   Mary Magdalene goes to the tomb; the stone has already been rolled away; she goes to tell Peter and the other disciple that Jesus has been taken away; both go to the tomb, see the grave-clothes and believes that Jesus is risen.

20.11–18   Mary Magdalene at the tomb sees two angels, then Jesus; she is told not to touch him, but to tell the disciples that Jesus is ascending to the Father.

20.19–21   Jesus appears to the disciples behind closed doors; shows his hands and side, and sends them out to preach.

20.22f.   Jesus breathes on the disciples, 'Receive the Holy Spirit', and gives them power to forgive sins.

20.24–9   The story of Thomas. On the eighth day Jesus appears to the disciples along with Thomas; Thomas is to feel his hands and side; says, 'My Lord and my God.'

21.1–23   Jesus appears to the disciples beside the Sea of Galilee; converses with Peter; 'the third time' (verse 14).

Acts 1.3   For forty days Jesus appears alive to the disciples.

1.4f.   Jesus at table has told the disciples not to leave Jerusalem until they had received the promise (the Spirit).

1.6–11   The ascension; a cloud takes him from their sight on the Mount of Olives.

2.1–13   Pentecost; the coming of the Holy Spirit.

1 Corinthians 15.3–8	Appearances: to Peter; the twelve; over five hundred; James; all the apostles; Paul.

A WORD TO MUSLIMS

Before asking Muslims to look at the Christian faith it is necessary to indicate how much truth there is in their own religion as seen by a sympathetic Christian. The central point here is that Muhammad truly received revelations from God. The people of Mecca had had some contacts with Jews and rather fewer with Christians, and had formed vague ideas about these religions. They may have understood that these people believed in a divine being who had created the world, and possibly that he had spoken to the Jews through prophets. Muhammad probably meditated on some of these matters, and then after a time began to have experiences which he regarded as similar to those of the Jewish prophets. The words which came to him in these experiences he preserved, and they constitute the Qur'an as we now have it. Christians should regard Muhammad as correct in his belief, and therefore accept the Qur'an as truly a collection of revelations from God.

It is next necessary to emphasize, however, that the process of divine revelation to human beings is far from simple. God's revelations to Abraham, Isaac, Jacob and their descendants stretched over many centuries. The revelations which form the basis of the Old Testament were not complete revelations of divine truth, but were limited revelations meeting some of the needs of the generation which received them, but needing to be supplemented and occasionally corrected for later generations. The religion of the Old Testament is thus a growing and developing religion. The Christian believes that Christianity is a further development of the religion of the Old Testament, based on new revelations received by Jesus. As the religion developed from Moses to the early Christians some of the revelations became superseded and had to be dropped. One such was the command to Joshua and others to submit certain towns to 'the curse of destruction'; and this meant putting to death all the men, women and children in them, and sometimes also the animals. This barbaric practice was presumably justified by the conditions in which Joshua and the other early commanders found themselves, but it cannot be considered in more civilized societies.

The revelations received by Muhammad brought to him and his followers, the first Muslims, a basic knowledge of God and of his dealings with human beings. In the following centuries this knowledge spread to the millions of people who accepted Islam; and this is to be seen as an outstanding contribution to world history. The question must be asked, however: Does the Qur'an give the full and final truth about God, or is Qur'anic truth open to something additional? Christians take the latter view, namely, that it needs to be supplemented, and also occasionally corrected. There is, of course, already some knowledge of Judaism and Christianity in the Qur'an, but it reflects the views of the Jews and Christians whom Muhammad and the earliest Muslims had met; and these people do not seem to have had a full and proper knowledge of their own religions. Thus, although the account of the birth of Jesus in the Qur'an (19.22–34) differs from that in the New Testament, something like it was apparently held by certain heretical Christian sects. Moreover, while the Qur'an gives a true account of the views of some Jews and Christians, and speaks of Jesus as a great prophet (which he was), it contains nothing about the highest and most developed forms of these religions. A Christian may therefore claim that his religion, when properly understood, has something to add to the beliefs about God revealed in the Qur'an.

Something must be said about the verse (4.157) which seems to deny the death of Jesus on the cross. That Jesus died on the cross is one of the most certain facts of all history. A possible translation of the verse is: 'they [the Jews] did not kill him, they did not crucify him, but it was made to seem so to them'. The primary purpose of this verse appears to be to deny that the crucifixion was a Jewish victory, and this is a point Christians would accept. Some Muslim scholars have seen the difficulties regarding this Qur'anic verse, and have tried to deal with them. One of these is Mahmoud Ayoub in an article entitled 'The Death of Jesus: Reality or Delusion' (*Muslim World* 70 (1980), pp. 91–121). His main conclusion is: 'The Qur'an is not here speaking about a man, righteous and wronged though he may be, but about the Word of God who was sent to earth and returned to God. Thus the denial of the killing of Jesus is a denial of the power of men to vanquish and destroy the divine Word, which is for ever victorious.'

Muslims should also consider whether some parts of the Qur'an have not become outdated, since most Islamic communities are now more civilized than the community in which the Qur'an was originally revealed. Thus the amputation of a hand as a punishment for theft, which is prescribed in the Qur'an (5.38), would no longer seem to be appropriate. I would therefore ask Muslims to look carefully at various presentations of the

103

Christian faith, including the one in this book, and consider whether there is not something which can be added to their Islamic beliefs, especially in the achievements of Jesus himself.

(A very sympathetic discussion of all the Qur'anic statements about Jesus is contained in *Jesus in the Qur'an* by Geoffrey Parrinder, 1965; latest edition, Oxford, One World, 1996.)